Heart's Compass Tarot

Heart's Compass Tarot

Discover Tarot Journaling & Create Your Own Cards

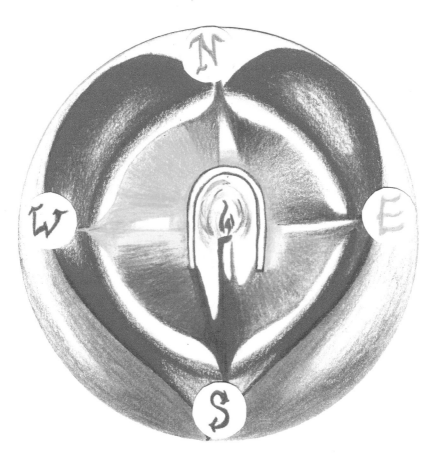

What happened, who am I now, who would I like to be?

Tania Pryputniewicz

TWO FINE CROWS BOOKS

Heart's Compass Tarot
©2021 Tania Pryputniewicz

Two Fine Crows Books
Ithaca, New York
twofinecrowsbooks.com

ISBN 978-1-7329521-6-4

Also by Tania Pryputniewicz
November Butterfly

For the four pillars of my tarot world:
tarot mentor Quan Tracy, reiki muse Bonnie,
tarot steady Mary, and the musician of my heart, my father Stephen

"The years of which I have spoken to you, when I pursued the inner images,
were the most important time of my life."
—Jung, C.G.

CONTENTS

FOREWORD 9

INTRODUCTION 11

A NOTE ON CHANGE 14

HOW TO USE THIS TAROT WORKBOOK 16

PART I

TAROT BASICS AND PLAYSHEETS 19

THE STRUCTURE OF THE TAROT 20

PART II

SIX CARD DEEP DIVE 31

THE FOOL 32

ACE OF CUPS 41

ACE OF WANDS 47

ACE OF DISKS 53

ACE OF SWORDS 59

THE MAGICIAN 65

TAROT JOURNALING QUESTIONS FOR MINOR ARCANA, PEOPLE CARDS,

    AND MAJOR ARCANA 71

MINOR ARCANA TAROT JOURNALING QUESTIONS ... 72

PEOPLE (COURT) CARDS TAROT JOURNALING QUESTIONS ... 81

MAJOR ARCANA TAROT JOURNALING QUESTIONS ... 84

CREATING YOUR PERSONAL TAROT INTERPRETATIONS OR KEYS ... 87

PART III

TAROT EXERCISES AND LAYOUTS 89

PERSONAL CARDS AND FULL DECK 90

PART IV

Tarot-Based Essays, Poetry, and Art Exercises   109

Tarot for Two   110

A Heart's Compass Note on Tarot and Fear, FAQs   130

Tarot Resources and Bibliography   133

Acknowledgments   136

About the Author   138

FOREWORD

Reading *Heart's Compass Tarot*, it's difficult for me to believe that before meeting Tania Pryputniewicz, I had no interest in tarot. I knew some who dabbled (my word) in tarot as a part of the alternative New Age world swirling around Northern California, but I shied away from tarot and anything I thought of as occult. I told anyone who asked that I was not a spiritual person, that, in fact, I even hated the word "spiritual."

That changed when Tania and I attended a writing retreat sponsored by A Room of Her Own Foundation in August 2011, a group of women gathering in the high desert at Ghost Ranch made famous by the painter Georgia O'Keeffe.

Each night, with the sun going down behind the mesas, a few of the writers read from their work. The night I finished my own reading, Tania came up to introduce herself. She told me she recognized one of my poems, and we searched our memories to find a connection. We finally realized we'd met years before at another writer's conference at which I'd read that same poem. At that time, Tania had asked me to submit the poem to a blog she coauthored, but I had simply thanked her and promptly forgot about it.

That duo of chance meetings was just one of the many serendipitous—and for me unnerving—interchanges and intersections that had occurred that week in New Mexico. Tania called it synchronicity. By the time we flew back to California, unexpectedly on the same flight (another synchronous event), I realized we had created a friendship that would last long beyond the retreat.

Sitting in the Albuquerque airport, we reminisced about some of our experiences at the retreat, such as the intense group discussions about writing and spirituality and religion and the soul, meditation sessions and walking the labyrinth of stones laid out in a spiral. All that made me uneasy, but I had to admit my carry-on bag was filled with rocks and pebbles I had collected on my hikes around Ghost Ranch. I confessed to creating altars of the bits and bobs I collected —even though I was not spiritual in any way.

Tania encouraged me to take photos of my altars and blog about them. Unsettled but intrigued, and because all that week I had been guided by the "spirit" of Georgia O'Keeffe and the inspiration of those creative women, I took Tania's advice.

It would not be the last time Tania invited me to explore new ideas. The first time she offered to do a tarot reading for me, I was intrigued to find out what might happen. From the little I understood of tarot, I knew some readers used the cards to divine the future, making predictions of upcoming events—predictions I wouldn't have believed. I was relieved to find that Tania interpreted tarot in a deeper way.

She directed me to close my eyes, shuffle the cards and then spread them out before choosing the ones which seemed to call my hand. When the cards were revealed, the brightly colored pictures, the suits of fire and earth, water and air, the descriptions of Fool and Magician, Star, Moon and Sun, all seemed rooted in the world of folk tales and stories of long ago. How could I not be charmed?

Tania described the meanings of the cards I had chosen and asked me to find connections between the words, their symbolism, and my own life. As she put it, she wanted me to "become my own oracle," providing my own interpretation and its meaning in my life. She didn't push me to believe a particular idea was correct if I couldn't relate to it. Instead, she showed me how to use tarot as an exploration of my inner self.

The most important tarot reading Tania led me through was based on questions I posed about the book I was writing about my relationship with my father.

We went through our familiar ritual. Then as Tania and I studied each card, she posed questions about my writing, asking me to find my own truth about the wisdom the card offered. I came away with a greater understanding of some of the issues I faced in my relationship with my father as well as a greater understanding of what I wanted to write. I've read the notes Tania made of that reading many times to help me delve deeper into my work.

When I read over this workbook's table of contents, I realized that I had completed most of the exercises included here. I've explored tarot with Tania in many different ways, using the cards to open doors to my writing, helping me deal with questions I pondered, creating poems and stories using cards as writing prompts. And although I've never considered myself a visual artist, one of the most valuable experiences I've had was creating my own tarot cards. Using Tania's exercise, I learned to overcome my insecurity and found joy in taking up my colored pencils to become a creator in a different way, forging a new path.

I am excited that Tania has compiled her teachings into *Heart's Compass Tarot*. You, the reader, will now be able to take your own journey with it as your guide. Whether you're new to tarot, as I was, or someone who wants to continue walking the tarot road in new ways, this book will provide you with plenty of inspiration. I wish you tarot blessings.

Lisa Rizzo, author of *Always a Blue House* and *In the Poem an Ocean*.
Portland, September 6, 2020

INTRODUCTION

Whether you are tarot curious, tarot savvy, or somewhere in-between, I welcome you to *Heart's Compass Tarot*, an approach to using tarot as a life compass and a mirror of the soul. This workbook is for all who wish to deepen the relationship to the self through journaling to tarot cards, journaling to discover personal symbols for tarot card creation or meditation, and improvisations in tarot-related art, poetry, and tarot layouts.

Hands to heart, eyes closed, we begin each encounter with the cards by taking a few deep breaths and feeling the ever-present companionship of our own two hands warming our heart, bringing us to the present moment.

You are the oracle. You just may not know it yet.

We often forget, under life's onslaught, to be our own best friend. Maybe you are depleted, exhausted. Maybe you are overflowing with opportunities but at a loss for how to choose your next step. Wherever you are, you don't need anything but yourself, an open mind, an open heart, a pencil or pen, and this workbook.

Tarot journaling helps you connect your life experiences to the imagery on the cards. Everything begins from that.

Every tarot deck is structured around the four elements— water, fire, earth, and air. How do you love, feel, or experience emotionally? (Water, or the Ace of Cups) How does your creative life-force power you? (Fire, or the Ace of Wands) How do you care for your body and manifest abundance? (Earth, or the Ace of Disks) How do you think, communicate and dream? (Air, or The Ace of Swords) How we use these four elements—or how we are blocked from using them—makes up the story of our lives.

This workbook helps you gain clarity about your personal narrative by establishing a journaling practice alongside the study of the tarot. This is an unfolding, not a quick fix, but a process of deep mining and insight. One of the most beautiful benefits of giving oneself over to this kind of steady introspection is a renewed ability to bring your awareness more fully into the present moment.

Be in that moment, hear yourself think, begin to heal by forgiving yourself and others, and connect to your dreams again.

Journaling connects our minds to our hearts and sets up the conditions for self-awareness. When you add tarot as a source of inspiration for your journaling practice, you enter a vivid landscape of depicted scenarios, human characters, and archetypal figures and energies to explore.

The tarot journaling questions in this book are meant to help you align with your heart's desires. You can point the arrow of your journaling inquiry into the past (experiences you've already lived, as related to a card) or into the present (what you see in your present life that mirrors the card) or even peek into the future (what you wish for, or what you intuit this card is saying about how to pursue your dreams).

Ruminating, journaling, and responding with art begin to lead organically to understanding your own world of symbols and personal expression in relation to the tarot card you are studying.

Gradually, through this process you will become aware that you are your own oracle. Through tarot journaling you discover the symbols specific to your own life, which can then be used as a focal point for further writing, meditation, or personal tarot card creation to help you imagine and create your future.

In addition to tarot journaling, in this workbook you'll learn simple tools such as how to create a Tarot Timeline of your experiences with the cards, and how to take your "tarot eye" into your daily life to see living expressions of the tarot energies in the people and situations you encounter. You'll also find steps for tarot card creation and a handful of playful exercises, from how to begin a tarot practice with a friend to writing tarot haiku.

Here's a quick view of the workbook's main sections (you'll find a more in-depth look in the "How to Use this Workbook" section at the end of this Introduction).

— Tarot Basics: Playsheets for Preparing to Engage the Tarot

— Six Card Deep Dive: The Four Elements, the Fool, and the Magician

— Tarot Exercises and Layouts Based on Your Personal Cards and the Full Deck

— Tarot-Based Essays, Poetry, and Art Exercises

— Afterword: A Writer's Journey Through Tarot and Tarot Resources

Tarot's Royal Road unfurls perpetually before us, paved by every past student and scholar of the tarot, always morphing just as our needs and consciousness do, inviting us to engage the tarot in ever-evolving ways and lay down our own bricks on the road for those who come after us. Join me and place your feet beside mine on the path.

Artist: Kalli James

Trust your need to quest
Moon's ceaseless silver bounty
Weightless, lights your path

A NOTE ON CHANGE

If you've picked up this workbook, chances are you're ready to step into your personal power with authenticity and joy in a world that is constantly changing. Many of us wish to understand the narratives within us to gain greater perspective on reality and our place in it. We ultimately wish to effect change— rewrite the narratives around us and create new realities. Envisioning new pathways for our communities and the world begins with one person quietly doing the work of finding and expressing their own power and creative agency.

Change is often beyond our control. We are born to particular parents in a particular region into a particular culture with its gifts and challenges. As we grow from child to adult, we learn either formally or informally. We fall in and out of love with friends, lovers, mentors; we marry and start families or walk solitary paths. We move to new cities, new schools. We graduate, divorce, or stay married and find ourselves in midlife wondering who we are, not only to others, but to ourselves. Some of us end up raising children while caring for a dying parent or loved one.

No matter the face of change, even when positive (a new career, a newborn, a new lover, an opportunity to start over), we often feel trepidation. With its centuries-old structure, tarot helps us look at the human psyche and human problems. The deck shows us the dance of human experience and soul growth from innocence (like the Fool card) to a joyful state of awareness and perspective as an active, awakened member of the community (like the World Card). Tarot journaling can help us be clear about who we are and what we have to bring to the table.

Using the Heart's Compass Approach, you'll ask, *What happened, Who am I now, and Who would I like to be?* Looking at a card in this multilayered way and plotting your pivotal life events along a Tarot Timeline helps you make peace with the past, appreciate where you are now, and envision what you'd like to bring into your present (and thus, shape your future).

Inner tarot work starts by drawing one card and journaling to the questions above.

Outer tarot reflection continues when you take your tarot eyes out into the world and live with greater awareness by playing a little game with the world, looking for expressions of the card in the world around you, and journaling about them.

No matter what life throws at us, we have the means to reconnect to what gives us joy when we turn inward to our dreams and the visual symbols that resonate for us personally. What might feel magical is simply harnessing our internal energies in synergy with external opportunities.

It can feel daunting, depending on what you have experienced before. But you begin with one card at a time. May your tarot journey lead you to see your worth, your joy, and your potential, and lead you to understand that you are an irreplaceable player on the world stage, and that we all benefit from having you express your gifts.

How to Use This Tarot Workbook

Here are some of the tools and what they can yield for you. Depending on your prior experience, you may decide to skip over the playsheets, though there's value in journaling to the questions no matter how long you've been engaged with the tarot. Feel free to jump to any section that appeals to you—there is no need to travel through the book in a linear fashion nor any predetermined amount of time for each chapter—take as long as you like and linger where your curiosity and your joy leads.

Tarot Basics and Playsheets

These questions invite you to take stock of your relationship to tarot, including your choice of deck, study habits, and your experience with creating artwork if you become inspired to try your hand at tarot card creation. *Taking this step helps you establish or reconnect to your relationship to the tarot and how you'd like to approach studying the cards.*

Six Card Deep Dive

What Happened, Who Am I Now, and Who Would I Like to Be

Here you put yourself in dialogue with a tarot card by considering your experiences of yourself, other people, and the world. The six cards chosen for this section will give you a solid introduction to the tarot's structure and will enable you to continue exploring the rest of the deck on your own. You'll meet the Fool (The Beginner), the four elements as expressed in the four Aces, and the Magician, who artfully blends and expresses those four elements. In each Deep Dive Chapter, after an introduction to the card, you will begin to consider which facets of your personality and life might evoke or embody the card, and then journal about those connections.

Tarot Timeline Creation

After journaling, you will plot a Tarot Timeline of your own lived experiences one card at a time on either a long piece of butcher paper or as notes in a journal you keep for your tarot studies.

This step anchors your understanding of where you've come from, your patterns, and what you've lived in relation to each card. It prepares you to meditate upon your own personal symbols or to make your own personal tarot cards. It aligns you with who you are so that you can better envision where you'd like to head and what you'd like to bring into your life.

Cultivating your "Tarot Eye" and taking it into the world

Joyful, playful, active witnessing.

As you go about your daily life, you are looking for examples that express your tarot card in real life (as if the world were a three-dimensional tarot deck and you and others are a living expression of the tarot). This kind of tarot study sends you on two types of treasure hunts.

Treasure hunt in your home

Search for anything that relates to the card you are studying. For example, working on the Fool card, a travel brochure on your refrigerator might remind you of the trip you took to Bali, or you may have a photo of your family on a hike that turned out to be way more vigorous than any of you expected. Each week you'll place the most joyful of those reminders in view on a special shelf or location. You'll be invited to journal about the items you chose.

These steps serve to anchor your understanding of where you are now to the energy of the card and the ways you may already have manifested its physical aspects.

Treasure or omen hunt in the outer world

Search for anything that sparks a connection to the card. Record in your journal what you noticed as you went about your day, and how it seemed to relate to the card.

This action step creates a dialogue with the card in present time.

Personal symbol search and tarot card creation

This involves daydreaming, drafting, sketching, doodling—"arting." While connecting to a card you are studying, you begin to think about and journal about the personal symbols that resonate for you. With the tarot card you are studying in mind, you ask, "What would I like to welcome into my life through this card?"

This step helps you begin to center and land on your own symbols for continued tarot journaling, meditation, and the creation of your personal tarot cards.

Continued tarot study

Stay connected to your personal tarot card. Using the compass of your heart, navigate by means of daily choices towards "the next right action" on the path of your dreams as you distill your deepest vision of joy and agency for yourself. Continue tarot journaling about these insights.

This follow-up step allows you to use your own personal tarot card as a visioning tool to attract your next steps and dreams.

Here you have a chance to play with a full tarot deck, to use it as a mirror to explore other aspects of your life (for example, your relationship to parents— see the Empress and Emperor), the ways you relate to yourself and others, and even create your own layouts.

This step allows you to deepen your engagement with the tarot and come to know more about yourself.

TAROT IMPROVISATIONS

These tarot-inspired essays, poetry, and art encourage you to take your tarot journaling/ meditation work into other creative forms.

AFTERWORD: A WRITER'S JOURNEY THROUGH TAROT

A personal look at how tarot entered my life and the years of teaching tarot classes that formed the basis of this workbook.

TAROT RESOURCES

A note on common fears associated with tarot study and a suggested reading list of tarot books and tarot-related literature follow the afterword.

If you decide to continue creating a full tarot deck, you'll find a list of introductory questions at the end of The Six Card Deep Dive chapters to guide you through cards two through ten, the rest of the Major Arcana, and the People cards based on the *Rider-Waite-Smith* deck and my tarot library of decks.

On the other hand, you may find a lifetime of joy working with the powerful initiation energies of the Aces. The New Year is a beautiful time to revisit your Aces and consider making a new one. Or you may have landed on a symbol that remains potent for a lifetime. There are no rules.

If you are someone who creates best in community, see the "Tarot for Two" chapter for suggestions about how to work with a tarot buddy.

PART 1

TAROT BASICS AND PLAYSHEETS

The Structure of the Tarot

A tarot deck is comprised of 78 cards and can be divided into three main categories or types of cards— Major Arcana (big secrets; soul energies), Minor Arcana (little secrets; daily life scenarios), and People Cards (personalities/skills; how we express ourselves). Here's an overview of how the entire deck itself is structured using the *Rider-Waite-Smith* deck as an example.

Major Arcana: Big Secrets

The 22 Major Arcana (big secrets and soul growth opportunities) are cards that speak to our *soul path* from innocent beginner (The Fool Card) to fully realized mature adult (The World Card), incorporating other cards like the Emperor and The Empress (male and female archetypal energies), The Tower (inevitable and all-encompassing change or insight we can't unsee), the Wheel of Fortune (riding the wheel of our earned bounty upward or descending toward arid periods) and more.

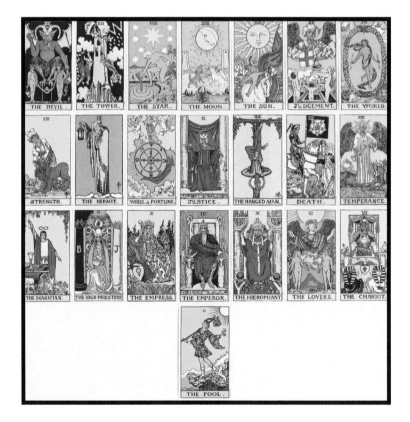

The 40 Minor Arcana (little daily secrets and growth opportunities) are cards that show us our *physical self's path*, how we actually move through daily life. These cards are organized by the *four elements*, and each set of ten scenarios in the Minor Arcana cards is anchored by its initiating Ace.

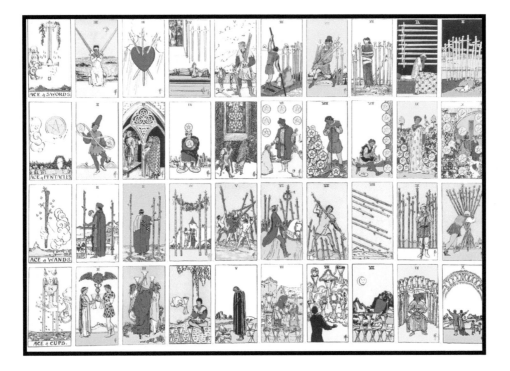

THE FOUR ELEMENTS

The four elements form the foundation of every human incarnation. They are—

The *Water* that courses through oceans, rivers, and lakes, falling from the sky, and the tears of emotion that spill down our cheeks in sorrow or joy, love or anger.

The *Fire* that greets us as at sunrise every day in our Sun, and the solar fire of the solar plexus, seat of the will, moving us to risk and to connect. This life-force within powers our creativity, decision-making, and our willpower.

The *Earth* we stand on and draw nourishment from, the body we inhabit, the plants and animals, the ways we work, prosper, and manifest abundance.

The *Air* we breathe, the inner mindscape of ideas and dreams, the intellect, intuition, and how we articulate the invisible (our goals, our inner realities) with words.

The 40 Minor Arcana cards are organized in groups from Ace to 10 in each of the elements described above. They present us with *scenarios depicting daily challenges and opportunities*. In summary, they show us lessons of the heart (water, Ace of Cups); the will (fire, Ace of Wands); the physical life in the world (earth, Ace of Disks); and the mind (air, Ace of Swords).

PEOPLE CARDS

The 16 People or Court cards are also organized by the four elements (water, fire, earth, air). They show us *the masks, aspects of ourselves, or personalities we inhabit* as we express a particular emotion, desire, thought or action in daily life. People cards are organized from learner to full adept, showing the degree to which the fullest expression of each element has been mastered. As a whole, the linked images and people of a tarot deck are shown relating to other people, the world around them, and their own souls.

The whole tarot deck can be thought of as a composite human being representing the possible ways we could express ourselves on the body, personality, and soul levels. Or, in another metaphor, the tarot is like a museum. We can enter it in any state of emotional, spiritual, physical, or mental development. Each card gives us artwork to contemplate, one scene at a time. Each element has external embodiment in the world around us and internal embodiment in our own bodies. Each offers us external tools and ways to deepen our agency by connecting them to our inner skills.

TAROT NUMBERS

The deck is also organized by numbers, each with a particular meaning. The Aces are the initiating card in each suit that afterwards proceed from 2 to 10. For reference, here's a quick overview of the numbers and traditional associations. 1— initiation, beginning, 2— balance, 3— synergy/synthesis, 4— foundation/structure, 5— conflict, 6— triumph, 7— inner lessons, 8— change/inspiration, 9— completion/culmination, 10— leaping off point/transformation.

In this workbook, we begin with the 0, The Fool—both beginning and end, encompassing all other numbers.

We then focus on the Aces (0s or 1s, in each suit) and the Magician (1).

Each Minor Arcana card is linked numerically to the Major Arcana card that bears the same number. (There are many other areas of association, such as astrological correspondences; take a look at the bibliography for further reading suggestions.)

EXPLORING YOUR RELATIONSHIP TO TAROT

Purchase at least one tarot deck for basic study and reference. I recommend the *Rider-Waite-Smith* because of its purposefully chosen pictorial representations and its history. Tarot is a living language and a conversation among symbols constantly evolving across centuries. You could liken the *Rider-Waite-Smith* deck to a cast iron pot that has been seasoned for many years.

Once you become familiar with that deck and the basic structure of the tarot, it's fun to seek out additional decks that resonate with you. Each tarot deck maker interprets the cards and the basic tarot structure through their own lens, just as you will when you begin making your own cards. Please listen to your own intuition as you explore decks—let the artwork call to you, choose the deck that feels right for you and gives you joy.

FREEWRITING

Throughout this workbook, we will use the process of freewriting for our tarot journaling. Freewriting means simply that you write without judging what comes from your pen, allowing your hand to move freely across the page without editing or crossing out your work.

Here are a few questions to begin your tarot journal dialogue—

What role has the tarot played in your life up until now?

What do you like about the imagery in the tarot decks you have encountered? Write about decks you have worked with or seen. Consider symbols, colors, story, cultural depictions, and the art forms used in the decks.

What would you like to learn through tarot study?

Which area of your life or aspect of history or culture are you drawn to exploring? There are hundreds of decks, from Afrocentric to Celtic to Steampunk to Zen, so brainstorm for a minute about what you would like to explore—a specific culture? Nature? Goddesses? Or even cats (yes, there are cat tarot decks!)?

Do you like hybrid or multi-source works? Tarot Maravilloso (Spain) and others draw on fairytales, nursery rhymes, and children's books.

Pay attention to the area of life, personal ancestry, or time period in history you are already attracted to exploring. This will fast-track your relationship to the deck you choose to work with because of your natural affinity for the subject.

What have you felt was missing for you in what you see depicted in the cards? Write about specific cards—specific Minor or Major Arcana. Eventually, thinking about the archetypes or images you wish were represented will help you move into discovering personal symbols and creating your own tarot cards.

CARING FOR YOUR TAROT DECK

Silk, cloth drawstring bags, and scarves are some options for storing your tarot deck when it is not in use. Follow your heart as you choose a way to honor your deck and keep it sheltered when not in active use (for example, wrapping it and storing it in a wooden box with a lid, or in a covered basket). Some readers choose a central silk to use as a base cloth for readings, and some layer silks; you'll find your way to what pleases you. If you like handwork, hand-sewing the edges of your silks or cloths is a gentle way to meditate on your hopes and dreams for your tarot adventures.

BASIC METHOD FOR TAROT JOURNALING

In the Six Card Deep Dive chapters, you'll walk through a process for engaging with six specific cards. But if you wish to begin your tarot study now, here's an approach to studying the entire tarot deck, one card at a time. Pick out a blank journal you can devote entirely to tarot. Choose an interval of time (one card a day, a week or other interval) that fits the pace of your life.

The first time you work with the tarot will be like no other. You could liken it to the experience you have when you move to a new town. The very first time you drive through town, you take in the trees, the homes and front lawns; you look at the houses for clues about who lives here, what kind of people you might encounter. You notice what is blooming or dying in the gardens. You pass the bakery, the library, the town square and will always remember the color of the sky that day. Take that same innocence and open awareness to your deck, as you meet the cards one by one.

You'll find directions for two approaches below; feel free to use either method or a combination of them. Begin by pausing, closing your eyes, and placing your hands over your heart. Take a few deep breaths to center yourself in the present moment. After you've shuffled your deck to your satisfaction (either as you would before you play a card game or by simply mixing the cards with your hands as they lie flat on the table) select a card and follow the steps below.

OBSERVATIONAL APPROACH

Give yourself time to simply look at the card.

Let your eyes take in the colors, and notice if you are attracted to or repelled by the colors of certain portions of the card, or both. List the colors.

Notice the setting (color of sky, weather, landscape and vegetation, bodies of water, mountains, wildlife). If there is land, are there dwellings? List the flora and fauna.

Use the freewriting method when you are ready to answer the following questions:

If there is a figure, what action is the figure undertaking?

What do you think the central person or figure is thinking or feeling?

If your card does not feature a figure, look at the object/s. What is the object's "story?" Notice color, placement, and relationship to the rest of the card.

What is the hope or dream of the figure? What are they resolving or wondering?

When have you experienced what you see in the card? When have you encountered the objects or situations depicted?

Keeping the card in view, describe— What do you see in the card, and what do you notice in your body as you gaze at the card? You may also simply observe your reactions but writing them down leaves you a map of your insights for future reference.

Read what you have written so far and return to the original question or issue on your heart or mind when you started as you consider where the card leads you.

What is the card saying to you?

MEDITATIVE APPROACH

This method helps you put in place a rhythm of when, where, and how you respond to the tarot. These suggested cues help you step more deeply into your engagement and then help you bring yourself back to your present daily life.

Choose a location where you can set the card out (your dresser, desk, window ledge) anywhere in the house where you will easily see it (leave it out until you pick your next card for study). This keeps you in subconscious dialogue with the card through the imagery.

Working with the tarot helps you connect to your unconscious, which can awaken or respond to the images in the deck. (You can develop this conversation with the unconscious even more in the "Creating Your Own Layouts" section on p. 93— also see "Conversing with the Unconscious" on p. 105.)

Light a candle before you begin your tarot journaling. Honor the four elements. For example, a candle represents fire and air. Incense represents earth. Putting a flower on the table in a vase represents water and the heart. Set out your own objects that you associate with the four elements.

Give yourself a set beginning and ending time for your tarot journaling so you know when you will close the deep work of introspection.

Consider a grounding "closing" practice— blow out the candle, close your tarot journal, perhaps take a walk in nature; physical activity is very grounding.

Consider finding a friend to play with on the Royal Road of the tarot (either in person or online). We are often our own worst critics when interpreting tarot cards alone. A friend can bring levity and compassion to the habitual lens through which we see ourselves (see "Tarot for Two").

Choose a question or focus for the card before you go to sleep. How do your dreams answer? Respond in your tarot journal.

Try to come to the cards fresh, looking at a particular card and writing before you read the deck maker's interpretations. Tarot journaling gives you a chance to play and connect to your own experiences first, and to build the muscle of intuition.

After you journal, check out the deck maker's interpretation. Follow up with a second round of freewriting considering the deck maker's intended symbolism. Think of it as *their* take on their imagery and symbolism; your personal connection is equally valid because it is based in your own life experience. Improvising with the imagery will help you find your own symbols.

Creating a Tarot Timeline

You will create a Tarot Timeline in the Six Card Deep Dive Section of the workbook. Here's a preview—materials include a roll of butcher paper and/or a blank journal, pen or pencil, colored pencils or markers.

A Tarot Timeline is simply a physical scroll of paper on which you plot your own life events in terms of each tarot card you pull. It can also be kept in journal form. It's fun to use colored pencils for this work, but not required.

We will start with the Fool Card. I'll introduce some of the ways you could experience the Fool Card and then invite you to plot those experiences along a timeline. You can use this process to plot any of the tarot cards you work with in the future.

Below, you'll find an example of Amelia's Ace of Cups Tarot Timeline. For her, the Ace of Cups signified the first time she remembered swimming. It can embody feelings of joy, falling in love, or hardships—for example, when Amelia's father began drinking and had an affair that led to her mother moving out.

To create your Tarot Timeline, after you journal, select the most vivid or most pressing memories you have of the way you lived the card in the past, putting in the date and adding a few notes. If you continue to do this as you study the tarot, you will begin to get an understanding of when in your life you experienced or expressed each of the four elements (water, fire, earth, air) and their corresponding energies (heart/emotions, life force/creativity, body/money, mind/intuition). This will also lead you to see which tarot cards you feel little or no connection to, which is to be expected.

Filling in a timeline brings awareness of dreams you have forgotten or situations you wish to revisit in order to grow. The timeline helps you remember who you were when you were born, with your birthright energies represented by tarot's four aces. Using the tarot to heal, grow,

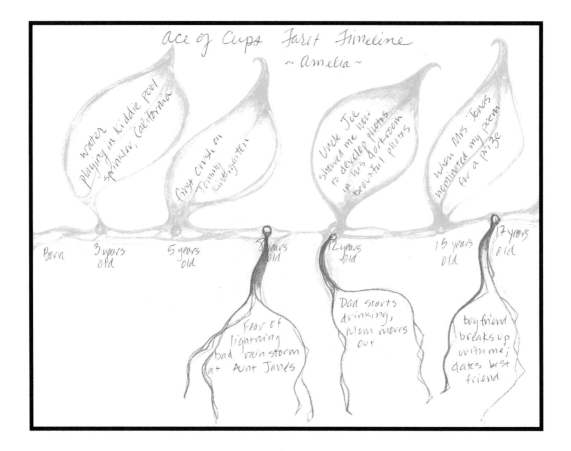

or shift doesn't replace modalities of healing like psychotherapy or medicine, but it is a very creative, image-driven way to work with the heart, will, body, and mind, engaging your intuition through visualization or meditating on a particular card to help bring about change.

Though you can certainly journal to create a written history, plotting the most significant memories and events in your life as images along a timeline often reveals patterns. And there's beauty in the metaphor of the empty ribbon of page stretching before you—the present moment and the future where you can use your growing tarot wisdom to decide where you'd next like to travel (figuratively or literally). If you happen to be a writer, you may uncover new material, brought vividly to the surface by your interaction with the tarot.

Coloring in your timeline provides a soothing way to ruminate and reflect. In the example above, Amelia placed her highlights or joyful experiences above the line (her harvest or tarot leaves and flowers), and her challenges or low points below the line (her root challenges) to symbolize what went into the compost of her past. Mapping both challenging and beautiful experiences gives us a fuller understanding of what makes up the fertile richness of the self we bring into the world at present. But there is no right or wrong way to make your timeline— follow your heart.

Exploring Your Relationship to Creativity

After tarot journaling to discover your personal symbols, you may wish to create your own tarot cards. This playsheet will also help you understand your relationship to creativity. It is very common to feel resistance, perfectionism, and outright fear when expressing yourself creatively, from writing to dancing to artwork. Entire books have been written on the topic. One of the best is Julia Cameron's *The Artist's Way*, a book you may wish to reference if you find these beginning questions open a Pandora's Box for you.

The questions below may help you open your heart to making art. Many of us came into the world freely expressing ourselves, but early relationships with others, even well-meaning others, from teachers to parents or siblings, may have stunted or blocked our natural creativity.

What do you remember about your own experience of creating or making art for the very first time?

When did you first create something you were proud to show or share, or even just enjoyed making for yourself? Write about your moments of joy, and any moments you felt blocked or felt an obstacle, whether that was an internal obstacle (self-doubt or fear), or an external obstacle (a person, a time constraint, financial constraint, etc.).

Who in your life inspired you to create or was supportive of your projects? Did anyone or anything stand in the way of your creative process? If so, write about those experiences. Try a dialogue now, speaking as yourself of today to that person or situation, in which you stand up for the younger self trying to create.

How can you best invite your playful self to this process of making cards?

Which mediums (collage, photography, combination, pastel, chalk, sketching, painting, clay, or more) are you comfortable using? Is there a medium you're drawn to trying for the first time for this project?

What are you most excited about when you think about making your own cards?

What are you most resistant to or concerned about as you think about making your own cards?

Art Materials and the Library

Give yourself plenty of time to choose the materials and art forms you want to use to create your own cards. Most especially, give yourself permission to change your mind. Look through the Six Card Deep Dive chapters (The Fool, The Aces, The Magician) where you'll see examples of personal tarot cards made by students. They chose a variety of materials and visual ways to represent their personal symbols or interpretations of tarot cards. There is no right way to make your own personal tarot cards; choosing a way that you enjoy is the goal. If you are new to making art or it has been a while since you made art, try heading to the public library, a beautiful free resource.

This is an adventure you can work into your routine as you work on your cards. The goal is to explore your particular language of color and shapes and design—what you are attracted to—and gather ideas for inspiration.

Go to the children's section of the public library, and look at the picture books. You'll find a wide range of art styles there from very sophisticated to simple collage styles, or photographs as illustrations. Librarians place an array of books facing out or prop them on shelf tops to attract the attention of children and their parents through the language of colors and graphic styles. Let yourself be a child again, selecting books that attract you.

Find three to five books with covers that look similar to your desired style of art (bring your journal or drafts of your cards with you, or bring photos of them with you on your phone).

Can you tell which medium the artist used?

Here's a list of possible art forms you could use to create your cards—

Collage

Photographs

Pastel

Watercolor

Acrylics

Pen and ink

Block Print

Sketching

3D exploration— sculpture

Combination of photo and collage or any of the above

You might ruminate while walking, thinking about your art process, or you might value a tactile, hands-on engagement with books, but you could also do this assignment by seeking out images online, on billboards, in magazines in a waiting room, or on the walls at your workplace.

Upon returning from your library trip, journal to the following questions to reconnect to your childhood relationship with stories, books, and art:

Were you read to as a child? What are your earliest memories of looking at storybooks or artwork? What kinds of stories and artwork appealed to you? Maybe you grew up hearing stories in an oral tradition. Which stories spoke to you as a child? List them; see if you can find them in book form and revisit them, or speak to the relatives (the storytellers and dream-keepers) in your family or in your community.

PART II

SIX CARD DEEP DIVE

USING TAROT TO DISCOVER YOUR OWN SYMBOLS

THE NEXT SIX CHAPTERS WALK YOU THROUGH

Overview of a tarot card

Tarot journaling questions

Tarot Timeline exercise

Home and world treasure hunts with your "tarot eye"

Personal symbol search for meditation and tarot card creation

MATERIALS

Tarot journal

Butcher paper

Colored pencils/markers

Art supplies for tarot card creation

From your purchased tarot deck—

Fool Card

Ace of Cups

Ace of Wands

Ace of Disks

Ace of Swords

Magician Card

THE FOOL

Blue boy, crimson girl,
Choose your Fool frame, plummet's lip
Satchel weighed with stars

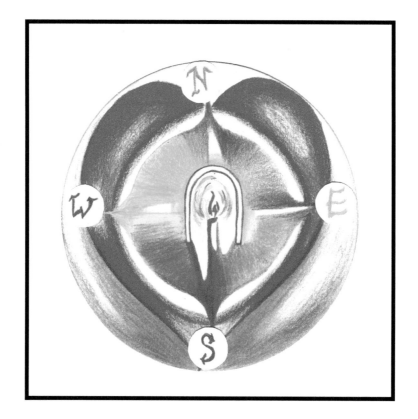

Follow the Compass of Your Heart

The Fool: Fearless Traveler, Joyful Innocent, Beginner of Journeys

The Fool is the joyful innocent, the beginner willing to set out anew. You are starting down a new path right now by taking up this workbook. Here we focus on the Happy Fool who trusts the universe. At first glance, the word Fool suggests someone being foolish or made a fool of. But foolish to whom? I invite you to use the compass of your own heart as you consider what it means to take a risk, to start over, to begin again with enthusiasm and optimism.

If you haven't done so already, set your Fool card out to use as a focal point, perhaps in the space in which you intend to write and create. Anywhere in your house where you can see the card throughout the week works fine. Take out your journal and read over your reflections about your favorite tarot decks from the playsheet, "Exploring Your Relationship to Tarot."

Words for The Fool

Beginning, Risking, Letting go, Stepping out, Embarking, Traveling, Entering, Leaping, Fooling, Joking, Non-conforming, Striding, Rebirthing, Relaxing, Trusting

Unfurl the butcher paper roll you've chosen for your Tarot Timeline, or open the journal you've set aside for your tarot reflections.

The Fool Tarot Timeline

Reflect and seek patterns through your past experiences of yourself, other people, and the world, in relation to The Fool. Start by taking the Fool card from the tarot deck you are using. Take a moment to place your hands over your heart. Close your eyes and take a few deep, slow breaths, allowing the heat from your hands to warm your chest. When you are ready, open your eyes and gaze at the card in front of you. Notice which portions of the card attract or repel you, taking note of the colors and images. When you are ready to begin writing, keep the Fool card in view and start by describing what you see. List the colors, objects, and figures in the picture; take note of the setting and landscape (mountains? desert? ocean?), the plants or animals, and the dwellings.

What did you first think about when you looked at the card? Did you notice any physical reaction to the card? Close your eyes and do an internal body scan. Answer any or all of the questions below, adding your own—

Think about the word "Fool." What comes to mind?

Consider times you set out on a journey. How did you begin—eager, innocent, joyful?

Also consider past pitfalls. Eileen Conolly, creator of the *Connolly Tarot Deck* and author of *Tarot: A New Handbook for the Apprentice*, speaks of the tarot in terms of crossroads and looking at past mistakes before moving forward— "The best swimmer in the world must know the depth before he makes his dive" (64). Where in your life could you "look before your leap?" Do this gently, in a highlight and a lowlight manner, or approach it neutrally—

What incidents, encounters, or people hold the most charge for you? What do you remember learning when you encountered or played out some aspect of the Fool or undertook a journey into the unknown? (Each card holds a spectrum of possibilities from positive to challenging. To end our inquiry on a positive note, write about the highlights last.)

Who in your family played either a positive version of the Fool (someone unafraid to look foolish in pursuit of their dreams), or a challenged version (someone others ridiculed)? What did you learn from them?

Are there other titles for the card that might express the energy of the Fool? Beginner, Innocent, etc.? What other words might you use to name your Fool card?

When in the past did you risk an adventure or action others might have considered foolish?

Plot your memories of your personal past Fool journeys on your Tarot Timeline— put in the date and select just a few key phrases that will jog your memory when you look at your timeline in the future.

TREASURE HUNT IN YOUR HOME

Search for anything that reminds you of the Fool card. Find physical objects or photographs from past adventures or experiences you recorded on your timeline (walking stick, favorite shells or rocks or other objects). Roam freely in your home and gather up your items. Place them around your Fool card on the altar space you have cleared. You may wish to take a photograph of your finished "Fool" collection of treasures and print it out for your journal. Take a moment to reflect on each item here— *I chose the following items on my Fool treasure hunt because...*

TREASURE HUNT, OR OMEN HUNT, IN THE OUTER WORLD

As you go about your day/week/month, search for anything that sparks your connection to the Fool— a train going by, the joyful burst of a boy in a line of bikers as he stands up to pedal, surging fearlessly into the wind. Record in your journal daily, connecting what you saw to the Fool. Did you see a billboard of someone leaping exuberantly into the air? Did you come across a magazine in the doctor's office with an image of an explorer? Maybe you overheard a conversation in which one person seemed to be rash and impulsive—this too can be an aspect of the Fool. Do a scan at the end of the week/month, and journal to this statement— *I witnessed the following expressions of the Fool card...*

PERSONAL TAROT CARD CREATION: DAYDREAMING, DRAFTING, SKETCHING, DOODLING—"ARTING"

Look in the children's section at the library for beautiful and varied examples of artwork and art methods (for examples of artwork or styles you might want to emulate, see "Art Materials and the Library" on page 29). Or your own bookshelves may hold examples of artwork you find inspiring. Move right into journaling to the questions below as you seek your own symbols for meditation or tarot card creation.

What adventure or new beginning would you like to celebrate or welcome into your life through the creation of your Fool card? What lessons or gifts or opportunities?

Which symbols and colors, images or representations most light up your heart when you think of new, joyful, fearless beginnings?

In many depictions, the Fool carries a satchel, often tied to the end of a stick he carries over his shoulder. What might be in that satchel? Or, when writing about challenges with the Fool card, what might be weighing down that bag? What is in there that could be traded in for something more useful for the next adventure? Everyone's past weighs down the Fool's bag differently, but for everyone there's an anchor of something we long to let go of, to set ourselves free. And for everyone there's also a corresponding anchor of someone inspiring us to soar. These characteristics are universal, though the specifics differ. What items or symbols does your Fool carry in his bag?

Step right into doodle/art/drawing/play.

Tarot Designs for the Backs of Your Cards

A simple way to engage with your chosen artform before you commit to creating your first card is to do some "tarot doodling" or sketching to create a design for the back of your deck. Spend some time in the bookstore or online noting the different designs deck makers use on the backs of their cards for ideas.

Trust and the Creative Process

Remember that the *creative process* means just that—*it is creative, and it is a process.* The important thing is to get your pencil or pen or paintbrush on the page and let yourself begin. Trust that the rest will come. Sketch, erase, try things; let yourself play. We build a bridge to our finished card one line or brushstroke or photograph at a time. Give yourself the freedom to draft as many versions as you like; think of your card as you might approach clay—you shape and reshape your clay, warming it in your palm, kneading it until it is warm and pliable. There's no need to get attached to the first version of your card unless you fall in love with it. The main thing is that the card gives you a sense of possibility and hope and joy.

Staying Connected to Your Personal Fool Card

Set your newly created Fool tarot card out where you can see and enjoy it. Continue to write in your journal, connecting your lived experiences to your card. What do you see in your outer life reflecting back to you that relates to your card? This may take some time. Leave your personal Fool card out and write once a day, once a week, monthly, or use it in a time capsule sort of way where you tuck it away for awhile and take it back out in a year. You might address in a freewrite— *"Dear Fool, I would like to risk…"*

GILLIAN'S FOOL CARD IN PROCESS

While making her Fool card, Gillian stayed open to creative exploration. Here is her final Fool card, although she kept adding colors and shapes to arrive at this version. Below you'll find her thoughts about her process—

This struggling bird (not at all phoenix-like) is trying to escape earthly ties while the last one seems to be more pinned to the earth and settled. I'm not sure it delivered on the Fool card...although I learned quite a bit about spirals...I drew and photocopied and cut out and pasted and drew over with a feverish delight, like a person possessed, like a fool! Loved it!

Gillian kept returning to her Fool card imagery and let herself enjoy the process, connecting her willingness to learn about spirals and her passionate and "feverish delight" to the Fool card energy. I invite you, like Gillian did, to trust your process and let yourself make as many versions of your card as you want.

STUDENT EXAMPLE 2— CARRIE'S FOOL CARD

Because Carrie also happens to be a poet, she chose to write her Tarot Key (or description of the card) as a poem, in which she beautifully defines the Fool card for herself in all of its complexity— "I am a pilgrimage of unfolding potentials." What a perfect way to invite the parts of herself that are learning and exploring. You'll notice she mentions the four suits; substituting depths for water and seeds for earth—"depths, seeds, air, and fire." You too can choose how to name your four suits and deviate from the more common four— water, fire, earth, and air.

CARRIE'S FOOL CARD CAPTION

The Fool is the picture of the keyhole in a stone wall, which is either the floor of a deep room OR the flat top of a tall building—either of which is built from other walls representing each of the four suits (depths, seeds, air, or fire).

CARRIE'S FOOL CARD INTERPRETATION OR KEY

my simplicity is underestimated or my complexity is misunderstood
sometimes I am a dreamer confusing folly for wisdom
the wall in front of me is actually a door or not
I am uncertainty itself:
the pause between the nexus of multiplicity
I am a pilgrimage of unfolding potentials
I expand my own limits
an ancient alchemy of play, intuition, synchronicity, abandon, and trust
my openness is never emptiness

Lisa also created a caption for each of her cards, and you'll see that she interprets her images as she goes. She calls her Fool "The Beginner," who has a body "pale green as young leaves, symbolizing birth and spring." Like Carrie, she wanted her Fool, The Beginner, to give us an image that would make us think of "potential." In her Tarot Card Key, Lisa acknowledges a common aspect we often encounter when beginning anew, which is fear, and addresses us directly— "We must trust we will find the light at the end. It doesn't matter our destination, but the journey we take."

LISA'S FOOL CARD CAPTION

The Beginner starts the ascent up a large set of stairs, filled with joy and reckless hope. Her body is pale green as young leaves, symbolizing birth and spring. The steps are steep and rocky without a handhold to steady her steps. She doesn't even notice. Instead she leaps higher and higher with her arms flung in the air in great abandon, reaching for the sun rising before her. A circle begins to unfurl, spiraling with potential.

LISA'S FOOL CARD INTERPRETATION OR KEY

The beginning of any new adventure can be fraught with fear. This card teaches us to have faith in ourselves. Each great journey begins with this climb towards what we seek. To reach the end, we must step off, begin up the stairs. We must trust we will find the light at the end. It doesn't matter our destination, but the journey we take. Like The Beginner, you must have the courage and freedom to try.

Now that you have completed your Fool card, we will look at creating our four Aces. These cards will take you on a joyful journey through the four elements of water, fire, earth, and air. Since birth, all of us have had a relationship with these elements. What if you could work with these elements intentionally to create self-acceptance and self-love, for the next leg of your journey?

Take a look at the Magician in your deck. In the *Rider-Waite-Smith* version of the Magician, you'll see all four aces on the workbench— cup (water), budding staff (fire), pentacle (earth), and sword (air), ready for the Magician to use to create. What will you create for your life using the elements?

You've noticed by now that the tarot cards in each element (or suit) are numbered from Ace (1) to ten and that each number corresponds to states and opportunities we experience in our daily life. We start with the 1s, the Aces.

If you decide to keep creating personal tarot cards 2-10, remember they will usually also bear the symbol you've chosen for your Ace or at least connect to it.

Take as much time as you need to discover your personal symbols. There's no predetermined amount of time for focusing on any of the Deep Dive chapters, layouts, or exercises in this workbook. Maybe you feel you already have a strong relationship with the suit of Cups as someone deeply in touch with your dreams, feelings, and emotions. But you would love to understand how others seem to earn money so easily, or enjoy nature, or dancing, or working out. In that case, you might wish to jump right to the earth (the Ace of Disks chapter) and start where you have the most questions. Trust yourself to begin at the place that makes the most sense to you and spend as much time as you need with your tarot play and tarot introspection process.

In the spirit of open-heartedness and love, let's begin our adventure with the Ace of Cups— gift of self-love, a chalice radiating with exuberant and uplifting love.

ACE OF CUPS

Self-love's Ace of Cups
Egret lands, folds outstretched wings
Heart rests between flights

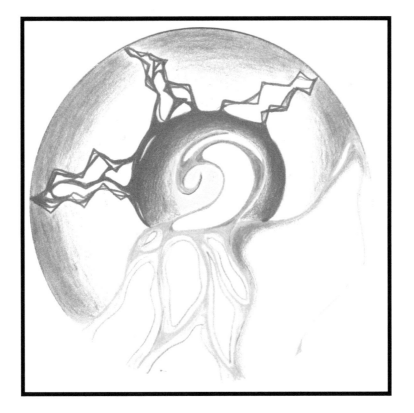

I allow my heart the full range of emotions
From volcanic core to seed-bursting as the sun
I invite my heart's waves from swell
To dissolving into the larger sea

The Ace of Cups: The Waters of the Heart

The Ace of Cups is the open heart, the clear heart, the trusting heart, the spiritual heart. This
is the Holy Grail sitting within the emotional nature...
—Angeles Arrien, *The Tarot Handbook*

What is the Ace of Cups?

Simply put, the waters of the heart, pure and loving, mirroring back our face to us when we peer
over the edge of the cup, an image of self-love. But self-love can be one of those fluffy terms we
shuttle back and forth to one another— "I know I should practice more self-love." What exactly
does it mean, and how do we know when we are living a life rooted in self-love?

Walking the husky one day, I watched an egret sail into view, land beside the bay, and fold
his outstretched wings onto his back. The feathered beauty of that moment was so peaceful. I
thought of the ways we extend love to our lovers, children, friends, as extending those wings.
But self-love might be like that sweet soft folding of one's wings onto one's back for a moment of
rest between flights. Can you remember a time you felt supremely content, let your wings fold
around yourself, felt joy encircle the heart? See if you can bring it into view.

Words for the Ace of Cups

*Loving, Healing, Balancing, Flowing, Appreciating, Feeling, Opening, Pleasing, Receiving, Accepting,
Grieving, Crying, Believing, Offering, Bathing, Wishing*

Ace of Cups Tarot Timeline

This is where you reflect and search for a pattern in your past experiences, considering yourself,
other people, and the world in relation to the Ace of Cups. Open your Tarot Journal, and unfurl
that roll of paper you've chosen for your Tarot Timeline. Take a moment to place your hands
over your heart. Close your eyes and take a few deep breaths, allowing the heat from your hands
to warm your chest. When you are ready, open your eyes and gaze at the card in front of you.
Notice which portions of the card attract or repel you. When you are ready to begin writing,
keep the Ace of Cups card in view and start by describing what you see. List the colors, objects,
and figures; take note of the setting and landscape (mountains? desert? ocean?), the plants or
animals, and the dwellings.

What did you first think about when you looked at the card? Did you notice any physical
reaction to the card? Close your eyes and do an internal body scan. Answer any or all of the
questions below, adding your own—

*Write about a time in your life 1) you allowed yourself to feel loved by others, and 2) a time when
you remember feeling joyfully at peace in solitude, aware of your intrinsic value as a human being.*

*In contrast to the usual bursting-with-light Ace of Cups imagery, sometimes our experiences of
self-love come unexpectedly at low points in our lives. What challenging situations have changed your
heart's map? Enlarged your understanding of love?*

You may also wish to write about self-love and how you learned about it from some other person who actively practiced self-care and self-love in an Ace of Cups way. What did they teach you and how? Or conversely, how might you have learned from them because of their lack of self-love? Write about specific family members, specific friends, or specific examples from society or popular culture.

Each card holds a spectrum of possibilities from positive to challenging; to keep our inquiry positive, write about the highlights last.

Take a moment to think about other titles for the card that might express the energy of the Ace of Cups. What alternate phrases might you find for this energy— heart waters, union, etc.?

When in the past did you experience deep joy coursing through your heart and a sense of belonging within?

Plot your memories of past Ace of Cups journeys on your Tarot Timeline—put in the date and select just a few key phrases to jog your memory for when you look at your timeline in the future.

HOME ACE OF CUPS TREASURE HUNT

Conduct a treasure hunt in your home for objects, images, artwork, and/or books that remind you of the energy of the Ace of Cups. Do you have a pair of earrings you bought for yourself? A pair of gloves you love? A colorful scarf? Favorite shells or rocks or feathers from when you walked on the beach? Take a photograph of your "Ace of Cups" altar collection of treasures and print it out for your journal. Take a moment to reflect on each item— *I chose the following items for my Ace of Cups treasure hunt because…*

WORLD ACE OF CUPS TREASURE HUNT

Over the course of the week (or your chosen interval), look for the Ace of Cups out in the world, on billboards, songs on the radio, in gardens you pass, on magazine covers, on windowsills. Journal to the statement— *I noticed the following expressions of the Ace of Cups card…*

PERSONAL TAROT CARD CREATION

Daydreaming, drafting, sketching, doodling—"arting"— spend time journaling, answering as many of the following questions as you can to prepare to create your own Ace of Cups card—

Where in your life would you like to receive love? How can you invite the cup of love into your life?

Which symbols, colors, representations most light up your heart?

In which area of your life do you wish to start a new emotional beginning?

Where in your life would you next like to offer the Cup of your own Heart?

Make a list of persons, places in nature, objects, colors, food, or experiences you associate with giving and receiving love, and consider which of these you might want to use for your card.

Continue into color/doodle/paint/art play.

All of the Aces lend themselves to three-dimensional play. The Ace of Cups often features a chalice. Fashion your own three-dimensional chalice out of clay or papier mache. Or re-fashion an existing chalice by painting or decorating it in a manner that feels symbolic of your own lived experience of self-love, or of the experience of giving and receiving love you'd like to draw to you.

Address in a free write— *"Dear Dream Ace of Cups, I would like to open my heart to…"*

STAYING CONNECTED TO YOUR PERSONAL ACE OF CUPS CARD

Set out your card where you can see and enjoy it. What do you see in your outer life that relates to your personal Ace of Cups card? Continue to connect your lived experiences to the card in your journal. This may take some time. Leave your Ace of Cups card out and write once a day, once a week, or monthly depending on your chosen interval of time.

Carrie decided to label her suit of Cups "Depths." Her caption accurately describes the image you see on her card—a hand made of ladders, with a womb or heart at its center. She takes the human hand and extends its agency by turning the fingers into ladders, a beautiful way to show how we reach and climb through our life, fired by the heart, which is nested here in the hand like a womb, a nod to the way we come through the bodies of our mothers.

Carrie's Ace of Depths Key gives us the riddles of poetry to take us further into her imagery of the ladder fingers and the womb— "I become connection itself, a resonating / wave upon wave upon wave / a constant, a beating heart like a nurturing womb within" which is a lovely metaphor for the way self-love gives a vibrant example to others. When we love ourselves, others may be inspired to love themselves.

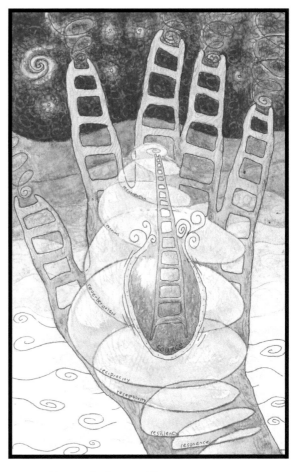

CARRIE'S ACE OF DEPTHS CAPTION

The Ace of Depths is the picture of an underwater heart/womb held in a hand made out of ladders.

CARRIE'S ACE OF DEPTHS INTERPRETATION OR KEY

as I seek my inner core, I begin to feed my own source
I become connection itself, a resonating wave upon wave upon wave
a constant, a beating heart like a nurturing womb within
I discover the emotional strength to climb upward
a reflective thing, a reflexive, recursive, spiraling path spreading ever outward
a resonating receptivity that can renew my sense of self
I grow more able to relate to others from this fulfilled state
and more able to help them see the source within them
this is the wisdom of the heart's healing

45

Lisa describes the way two hands hold her cup, its stars on the outside and streams of blue overflowing out of her chalice. In her Ace of Cups key, she continues her direct invitation and address to us, "With an overflowing abundance of love, you can become an integral part of a group. Welcome love in. Accept yourself, become an integral part of the human group." Lisa connects her self-love card to the larger heart of the community, extending her Ace to the human family.

LISA'S ACE OF CUPS CAPTION

Crystal goblet rises up out of the waves held by two hands emerging from the depths. Water flows up and over the rim, spraying out of the cup like a fountain, a great rush of water sparkling in the sun. The cup shines with stars.

LISA'S ACE OF CUPS INTERPRETATION OR KEY

This cup is a reminder of your heart. With an overflowing abundance of love, you can become an integral part of a group. Welcome love in. Accept yourself, fold yourself into the human circle. Keep growing and expanding; the gift of the cups will keep you buoyed. You are welcomed in. The air soft and fresh, day flooded with light. Give yourself that moment of self-discovery. Love radiating from the center out.

Tarot journaling questions to help you continue seeking symbols and creating personal cards for the suit of Cups, Wands, Disks, and Swords from Two-Ten appear at the end of Section 2.

ACE OF WANDS

Come little bee
Fill your pollen baskets
And fly where you will

As I pass through Earth's gardens
May my passions
Ignite the passions of others

ACE OF WANDS: FLOWER AND FLAME

May you flower and flame
—Barbara Rockman

Welcome to the Ace of Wands! Pure ignition! Spontaneous burst! Leaping into and out of the fire! Joyful self-expression! The Ace of Wands is the energy of fire, an image of our inner power, our fire, our creativity, our passion—or of burning away what is no longer needed to prepare our life for new gardens. Think of the way firelight dances up and back and flickers; in its burning you see the structure of the wood becoming incandescent. You see the form of the tree, you see its waterlines and root lines, even as it burns and gives off heat. We too must come to know our structures and what came before. As we prepare for any new project, we bring the structure of the past underneath us. This Ace of Wands invites all of your passion, burning to create, radiating power.

Another common image for the Ace of Wands is the budding limb of a plant, living proof of the secret strength drawn from the core of the earth, the sun above, and the rain to leaf and flower. This Ace invites us to experiment, innovate, and play, activating the third chakra, igniting the will and the power of light to express ourselves and burst fearlessly into bloom.

WORDS FOR THE ACE OF WANDS

Flowering, Burning, Discovering, Realizing, Revealing, Budding, Regenerating, Igniting, Surprising, Enchanting, Willing

ACE OF WANDS TAROT TIMELINE

This is where you reflect and search for patterns in your past experiences, considering yourself, other people, and the world in relation to the Ace of Wands. If you haven't done so already, set your Ace of Wands card out in your special spot. Take out your journal and unfurl the butcher paper roll of paper you've chosen for your Tarot Timeline, or open the journal you've set aside for tarot reflections. Take a moment to place your hands over your heart. Close your eyes and take a few deep breaths, allowing the heat from your hands to warm your chest.

When you are ready, open your eyes and gaze at the card in front of you. Notice which portions of the card attract or repel you. When you begin writing, keep the Ace of Wands card in view and start by describing what you see. List the colors, objects, and figures; take note of the setting and landscape (mountains? desert? ocean?), the plants or animals, and the dwellings.

What did you think about when you first looked at the card? Did you notice any physical reaction to the card? Close your eyes and do an internal body scan. Answer any or all of the questions below, adding your own—

Take stock of your Ace of Wands moments in your life. Consider your past, looking for times you felt powerful, creative, passionate and inspired. You might wish to do two separate scans; one for the creative aspect of the Wand, and one for your relation to passion —times when you felt joyfully free to express those aspects of the self.

When did you have an abundance of life-energy fueling a particular project or person? Was there a time you created something—a garden, an art project, a collaboration, or the making of a family?

When did you burn with unbridled spiritual or physical passion?

Or, as we've discussed with the other Aces, sometimes we uncover times when we felt blocked from the qualities represented by a particular card. Have you felt blocked or suppressed in your creativity or your self-expression? What situations or circumstances contributed to that blockage or suppression (for example, criticism from teachers, fellow students, parents, others)? How were you able to move out of the blockage?

Were there others in your life who freely experienced, expressed, or even shared with you their Ace of Wands exuberance and unbridled energy (family members, mentors, or in popular culture)?

What other titles might you use for your Ace of Wands?

When in the past did you experience a burst of creative fire that propelled you powerfully into a project or new enterprise or deep into a relationship with a collaborator or a lover?

PLOT YOUR MEMORIES OF PAST ACE OF WANDS JOURNEYS ON YOUR TAROT TIMELINE

Put in the date and select just a few key phrases to jog your memory for when you scan your timeline in the future.

HUNT FOR TREASURE IN YOUR HOME

Look for anything that reminds you of the Ace of Wands. Again, search the rooms, hallways, and even basement or garage, this time for images related to the Ace of Wands. Think of images of fire, energy, power, joy. What images do you have that remind you of that fiery state when you have landed on a new creative endeavor or project—when you were metaphorically "lit up" with joy and excitement—when you were bursting with the passion to create, already giving off light as you prepared to engage? Or burning with passion for a lover? Or consider images of sensual fire from body-based to nature-based imagery or art. Take a photograph of your finished "Ace of Wands" collection of treasures and print it out for your journal. Take a moment to reflect on each item— *I chose the following items for my Ace of Wands treasure hunt because...*

TREASURE HUNT OR OMEN-HUNT IN THE OUTER WORLD

As you go about your day, looking for anything that sparks your connection to the Ace of Wands. Lanterns lighting the bridge in the park at night? Bonfire at the ocean with friends? A clip of a powerful dancer or musician? Record in your journal what you saw in your daily life in relation to the Ace of Wands— *I witnessed the following expressions of the Ace of Wands...*

PERSONAL TAROT CARD CREATION: DAYDREAMING, DRAFTING, SKETCHING, DOODLING—"ARTING"

Spend time journaling to the following questions to discover your personal Ace of Wands symbol for meditation and creating your tarot card—

Define the Ace of Wands in your terms if you haven't already. Passion, creativity, self-expression, fire—what do these words mean to you?

What in your life is being undeniably brought into the light?

What in your life is burning away, freeing you artistically, physically, or spiritually?

What lights you up and refuels your creative juices? Where in your life would you like to be handed a gift of energy, enthusiasm, and inspiration?

What project or enterprise or creative undertaking do you long to let yourself enjoy?

If you uncovered obstacles to your creative or sexual expression in your writings about your past, consider the *Inner Child Cards* Ace of Wands butterfly imagery (artwork by Christopher Guilfoil) as you look to your future— "As we emerge from old wounds, we take on new colors and wear new wings of hope—much like the butterfly miraculously unspiraling from the dark cocoon" (Lerner and Lerner, 139).

What colors or wings do you see yourself metaphorically taking on or growing?

What are the obstacles to your sexuality, passion, power, or free expression in relation to yourself and others? In which area of your life do you wish to start wielding the Ace of Wands on your own behalf or on behalf of others?

What image could you create of the perfect tool to move through these obstacles?

Step right into color/doodle/paint/art play.

Address in a free write— "Dear Dream Ace of Wands, I would like to invite the heat of my creative passion to inspire me to…"

STAYING CONNECTED TO YOUR PERSONAL ACE OF WANDS CARD

Set your card out where you can see and enjoy it. What do you see in your outer life reflecting back to you in relation to your personal Ace of Wands? Keep journaling. Leave your Ace of Wands card out and write to it regularly.

Carrie chose to call her Ace of Wands "Ace of Fire." Her caption tells us that she's using the Greek letter Delta as a symbol. The symbol creates four triangular panels for her card yet presents a unified image. We are drawn to the scene in each partition, and so may not initially see the symbol. It's fun to think about ways to incorporate symbols that matter to you in your cards in this way. How might you use a symbol to divide up portions of your card?

In her poetry key, Carrie uses powerful "I" statements to speak as the card itself— "I strengthen and I build with my forge / and then I melt it all down and rebuild again and again" —referencing the stages of fire while highlighting the way fire acts both as a forge and a force that splits open seeds. She manages to convey the reductive and destructive aspects as well as the regenerative powers of fire.

CARRIE'S ACE OF FIRE CAPTION

The Ace of Fire is the picture of wildfire on the prairies, in triangles, like the Greek letter delta, for difference, the symbol of change.

CARRIE'S ACE OF FIRE INTERPRETATION OR KEY

I am the kindling that sacrifices itself to set forth the roaring flames
the flickering dance of fires' own fingers, a dancing, relentless hunger
when fueled, I am passion, am power
my path of destruction breeds chaos, and yet
this upheaval, this scattering disarray, it is required for a new ordering
I am the proving grounds of resiliency
the necessary condition for creative transformation
the vulnerability maker, the cracking-opener of hard seed casings
I cleanse away the stagnant underbrush with my scalding
I strengthen and I build with my forge
and then I melt it all down and rebuild again and again
this is the wisdom of change

Lisa's Ace of Wands poem is both caption and key. In her Ace of Wands card, we see the flames of creativity rising up from her pen which sprouts the early leaves of harvest at its top. Below the hand, we see the subterranean bounty of words waiting to be pulled up by the pen itself. She gives us the image of a candle as well as the heart to her Ace of Wands image. She connects the pen, tool of writer, to the heart driving the hand and the light coming off the candle.

LISA'S ACE OF WANDS POEM

burning bright
being lit by creativity
light and words flowing on the page
source of fire, the need to create
express deepest thoughts
comes bubbling up
a warmth spreading from the center
light the candle
rise in the dark
close to the heart.

Tarot journaling questions to help you continue symbol seeking and creating personal cards for the suit of Cups, Wands, Disks, and Swords from Two-Ten appear at the end of Section 2.

ACE OF DISKS

Strung from core through heart to sun,
Threaded by nutrient wick,
I trust the earth to support me

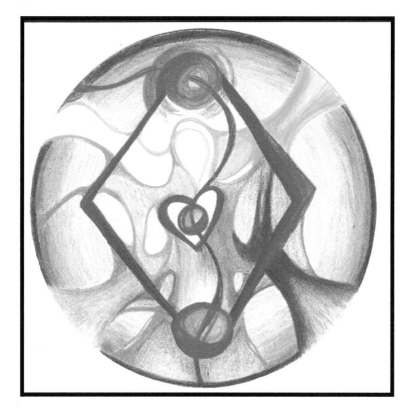

Rooted in my Earth inheritance,
Anchored by gravity and the heart,
I am tree, coin, body,
All prosperities large and small

ACE OF DISKS: MANIFESTER AND MUSCLE

...once you realize the Garden of Eden exists within you, you are free to leave it, taking it with you always as you create a new life.
—Rachel Pollack, *Seventy-Eight Degrees of Wisdom*

What is your relationship to Earth, to your belongings, to home and hearth, and to the ultimate house you came into, your body? Aces, anchoring at the root of each suit, are meant to remind us of gifts or blessings—both those we currently possess and those we may wish to open our heart, mind, body, and soul to receiving.

In the *Rider-Waite-Smith* version of the Ace of Disks, a hand emerges from the billowing clouds holding a golden orb. "Here," it seems to say, "Take this gift!" Traditionally the Ace of Disks is the coin itself, that which we exchange for goods and services. It is also seen as relating to material projects and to the body itself, made of earth, anchored by gravity to the earth. Our giving and creating hands afford us the means to create, to love, to shape, and to carry.

WORDS FOR THE ACE OF DISKS

Materializing, Grounding, Organizing, Sustaining, Prospering, Earning, Rewarding, Luxuriating, Securing, Sheltering, Composting, Succeeding, Producing

ACE OF DISKS TAROT TIMELINE

This is where you reflect and search for patterns through your past experiences, considering yourself, other people, and the world in relation to the Ace of Disks. If you haven't done so already, set your Ace of Disks card out in your special spot. Take out your journal and unfurl the butcher paper roll of paper you've chosen for your Tarot Timeline or open your journal. Take a moment to place your hands over your heart. Close your eyes and take a few deep breaths, allowing the heat from your hands to warm your chest. When you are ready, open your eyes and gaze at the card in front of you. Notice which portions of the card attract or repel you. Keep the Ace of Disks card in view and describe what you see. List the colors, objects, and figures; take note of the setting and landscape (mountains? desert? ocean?), the plants or animals, and the dwellings—

What did you think about when you first looked at the card? Did you notice any physical reaction to the card? Close your eyes and do an internal body scan. Answer any or all of the questions below, adding any of your own—

Scan through your past, looking for times you felt deep well-being, security, and prosperity. List the physical health, material wealth, objects, location, and other experiences that were associated with this feeling. Are you someone with "clothing karma," for example? That is, do people give you beautiful clothing? Disks can symbolize various kinds of wealth, whatever feels rich and fertile to you. Maybe you love art supplies or stained glass, and these gifts come to you through others. Wealth also includes the earth itself, its wildness, animals, plants, and gardens. It also includes the richness of our own bodies, anchored by gravity to the earth and made up of the elements of Earth. It also includes the richness of many friends. These are all tangible manifestations of wealth. We all have internal and external abundance, riches, goodness.

Consider this quote from Rachel Pollack's *Seventy-Eight Degrees of Wisdom*— "Earth in its completeness and solid reality, bears its own magic...magic will often remain hidden from us simply because we see its products as so ordinary..." (258).

What is your notion of home and hearth or home sanctuary? Which ancestors helped create your notion of home and hearth?

What is your relation to nature? Does it frighten you? Does it feel like the source of nurturance?

Where do you feel physically safe and where do you not?

How do you define wealth (mentally, emotionally, physically, spiritually)?

What is the "gold" in your present life?

Is there a gift in your present surroundings that you have overlooked?

If poverty was a recurring theme of the past, consider which dreams of prosperity—which longings to have or to manifest—remain with you today. Write about the part of yourself or the people in your life keeping the dream of manifesting alive.

Each card holds a spectrum of possibilities from positive to challenging, and to keep our inquiry positive, write about the highlights last.

What other titles might express the energy of the Ace of Disks, such as Ace of Trees, Ace of Coins, etc.?

When in the past did you experience an unexpected gift of prosperity, a promotion, a great feeling of safety and wellbeing, or deep joy over the physical manifestation of a particular dream or project?

ACE OF DISKS TAROT TIMELINE

Put in the date and select just a few key phrases to jog your memory for when you scan your timeline in the future.

HUNT FOR TREASURE IN YOUR HOME

Look for anything that reminds you of the Ace of Disks (a piggy bank, something that expresses your concept of manifestation, wealth, nature, the earth, disks, coins in artwork, or books on your shelves about prosperity). Take a photograph of your finished "Ace of Disks" collection of treasures and print it out for your journal. Take a moment to reflect on each item— *I chose the following items for my Ace of Disks treasure hunt because...*

TREASURE HUNT OR OMEN-HUNT IN THE OUTER WORLD

As you go about your day for anything that sparks your connection to the Ace of Disks. Continue to treasure seek during the week for images of the Ace of Disks out in the world— is there a sculpture, building, place, or representation of wellbeing, abundance, nurturance, or wealth you are drawn to? What do you see this week as you go to and from your ordinary errands?

Record in your journal what you saw in your daily life in relation to the Ace of Disks— *I witnessed the following expressions of the Ace of Disks...*

PERSONAL TAROT CARD CREATION: DAYDREAMING, DRAFTING, SKETCHING, DOODLING—"ARTING"

Spend time journaling to the following questions to discover your personal symbols for meditation and the creation of your card—

Define the Ace of Disks in your terms if you haven't already (define prosperity, wealth, abundance, manifestation).

How could you open your heart to receiving?

Is there a person/institution/situation in your life holding out a metaphorical golden orb for you to take?

In which area of your life do you wish to start manifesting particular forms or specific prosperities?

Make a list of persons, places in nature, objects, or colors you associate with prosperity and manifestation, and consider which of these you might want to use for your card. Step right into color/ doodle/paint/art play.

EXTENDED ACE OF DISKS PLAY

Fashion your own three-dimensional coin container or prosperity bowl, or play with creating your own coins or other miniature representations of a larger object you wish to manifest (clay, papier mache, etc). In fact, each card you make is an Ace of Disks manifestation— a tangible object representing your connection to your symbolic world.

Address in a freewrite— *"Dear Dream Ace of Disks, I would like to manifest...," "I would like my body to experience..."*

STAYING CONNECTED TO YOUR PERSONAL ACE OF DISKS CARD

Set your card out where you can see and enjoy it. Continue to write in your journal, connecting your lived experiences to your card. What do you see in your outer life that relates to your personal Ace of Disks card? This may take some time. Leave your Ace of Disks card out and write once a day, once a week, monthly, or use it in a time capsule sort of way where we you tuck it away for a while and take it back out in a year. It is up to you.

Carrie decided to name her suit of Disks
"Seeds." Her caption tells us we are
looking at a seed with its roots and its
reaching "towards potentialities." Notice
the layers of imagery in this card—
there is the seed, and also the vibrant
and varied green and orange globes of
what appears to be a tree or some other
harvest the seed may manifest. Carrie
has captured an image of potential in
both ways. What is your symbol for
potential? How could you layer your
card with your symbol for potential and
also that potential taking form in the
future?

In her poetry key, Carrie again
speaks as the energy of the Seed Ace
taking us deeper into her lovely now-
and-future imagery, "I am deep roots
cradling future seeds."

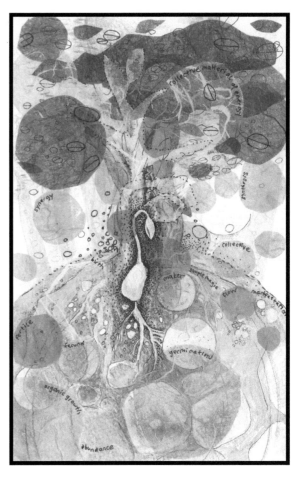

CARRIE'S ACE OF SEEDS CAPTION

The Ace of Seeds is the picture of a seed
with roots reaching downward while its
potentialities stretch toward the future.

CARRIE'S ACE OF SEEDS INTERPRETATION OR KEY

my potentiality is the embodied drive
of life-force undormanting itself
the unconscious flow of synergy of germination
I am the loss of self in making anew
the synthesis of fertile births and fecund lands
the collective manifestation of need
I am deep roots cradling future seeds holding riverbanks steady
the accumulated layers of life, of circles within circles, of patience incarnate
both the boughs providing shade
and the decaying litter feeding the next generation
the wisdom of the long view

Lisa's poetry again serves as caption and key. In her Ace of Disks card, we see the close-up of a blossom against the backdrop of a tree. Lisa has used the branches of the tree to place an affirmation, "As I grow, I prosper," one word per branch. In your card could you place an affirmation or message?

LISA'S ACE OF DISKS CAPTION AND KEY POEM

reconcile the idea of wealth and nature
as I grow I prosper
inner flowering and wholeness
possibility of unlimited movement
time of centeredness
abundance of your life
inner abundance
abundance of self

Tarot journaling questions to help you continue seeking symbols and creating personal cards for the suits of Cups, Wands, Disks, and Swords from Two-Ten appear at the end of Section 2.

ACE OF SWORDS

Guardian, witness
Seer, keeper of secrets
My turn to translate

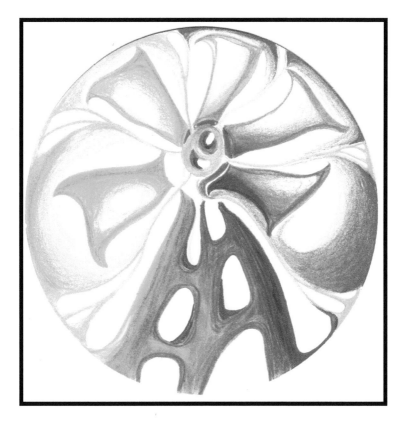

Wind wakes up my senses.
In it I feel my borders.
Of all oppositions
Beauty, art, joy

Ace of Swords: Clarifier, Winnower, Invoker

What is the Ace of Swords? Swords relate to the mind and thoughts—what we do not see. Thoughts, ideas, dreams, and visions, while not visible to the naked eye, are no less powerful, for they connect and bring action to bear on eventual manifestation. The Ace of Swords can refer to what is conscious and unconscious, a call to action, a tuning in, or words, spoken and unspoken. It invites us to clarify, though clarity can take multiple forms. To wield the Ace of Swords is to hone, focus, and attune. But it can also refer to cutting away what is no longer necessary, winnowing our thoughts to those that serve us best.

Words for the Ace of Swords

Intuiting, Inventing, Viewing, Thinking, Deciding, Questioning, Analyzing, Clarifying, Understanding, Perceiving, Breathing, Piercing, Discerning, Sorting, Bridging, Equalizing, Intellectualizing

Ace of Swords Tarot Timeline

Reflect and seek patterns through your past experiences, considering yourself, other people, and the world in relation to The Ace of Swords. If you haven't done so already, set the Ace of Swords card out in your chosen special spot. Take out your journal and unfurl the butcher paper for your Tarot Timeline or open your journal. Take a moment to place your hands over your heart. Close your eyes and take a few deep breaths, allowing the heat from your hands to warm your chest. When you are ready, open your eyes and gaze at the card in front of you. Notice which portions of the card attract or repel you. Keep the Ace of Swords card in view and start by describing what you see. List the colors, objects, and figures; take note of the setting and landscape (mountains? desert? ocean?), the plants or animals, and the dwellings…

What did you think about when you first looked at the card? Did you notice any physical reaction to the card? Close your eyes and do an internal body scan.

Answer any or all of the questions below, adding your own.

Scan through your past, looking for times you felt extremely clear and focused, as if everything had aligned and come into view, along with the ability to translate those insights into words (spoken or written).

What situations in your past brought you to new clarity or inspired a mental breakthrough in your ideas about your direction, purpose, dreams or desires?

Which person or persons in your past wielded an Ace of Swords ability to see clearly, analyze, or use words, thoughts, ideas or prayers clearly?

How have you used the Ace of Swords in relation to others? In relation to yourself? When were you on the receiving end of someone else's Ace of Swords clarity, for better or for worse?

What did you witness, learn, or what was revealed about the situation, or about the mind and how it works?

Consider educational settings, teachers and mentors, or other "bridge" experiences where you expanded and grew through learning, exposure to ideas, words, new perspectives, or dreams.

Each card holds a spectrum of possibilities from positive to challenging, and to keep inquiry positive, write about the highlights last. Take a moment to think about other titles for the card that might express the energy of the Ace of Swords card for you, i.e., Ace of Birds (perspective), Ace of Dreams.

When in the past did you experience mental clarity that you were able to translate into words or use to bring about greater clarity or resolution in a situation? Start by writing about other times you encountered the Ace of Swords.

Plot your memories of past Ace of Swords journeys on your Tarot Timeline

Put in the date and select just a few key phrases to jog your memory for when you look back at your timeline in the future.

Hunt for treasure in your home

Look for anything that reminds you of the Ace of Swords. This "airy suit" feels a little trickier, but persevere. Look for images in your home and your world. You can start with images of the sword if you are drawn to that, or images that remind you of the discerning power of the mind, intellectual clarity, or the power of words to articulate truth, such as a special pen or feather? Maybe you have an image of a spiritual teacher or writer or thinker you associate with enlightenment. Let yourself roam freely in your home and gather up your items. Place them around your Ace of Swords. You may wish to take a photograph of your finished Ace of Swords collection of treasures and print it out for your journal. Take a moment to reflect on each item— *I chose the following items for my Ace of Swords treasure hunt because…*

Treasure hunt or omen-hunt in the world

As you go about your day, look for anything that reminds you of the Ace of Swords— a building, temple, church, college or school where the play of ideas is encouraged? A coffee shop full of busy writers at their keyboards?

Record in your journal

What have you experienced in your life that related to the Ace of Swords? Did you attend a lecture or an open mic? Visit a counselor? See an osprey hovering high above the sea, focusing on its prey? Overhear a conversation in which one person cleared away a misconception for another? Scan through these entries at the end of the week or month, and journal to the statement— *I witnessed the following expressions of the Ace of Swords card this week…*

Personal Tarot card creation: Daydreaming, drafting, sketching, doodling—"arting"

Journal to the following questions to help you discover your personal symbol for meditation and tarot card creation—

Which of your typical thought patterns have best served you, and how might you represent them in this card?

Which parts of your intellect and mental processes do you wish to invite to grow?

Which symbols, colors, and representations feel intellectually stimulating?

In which areas of your life do you wish to start wielding the Ace of Swords? Make a list of persons, guides, places, objects, or colors you associate with a crystal clear state of mind and the ability to translate it.

Step right into doodle/art/drawing/play.

EXTENDED ACE OF SWORDS PLAY

You may be inspired to sketch, paint, sculpt or decorate an emblem for the mind, meditation, or other personal "power of thought" or intention symbol.

Address in a free write— *"Dear Dream Ace of Swords, I would like to invite your gift of clarity to help me see/reveal/focus on…"*

STAYING CONNECTED TO YOUR PERSONAL ACE OF SWORDS CARD

Set your card out where you can see and enjoy it. Continue to write in your journal, connecting your lived experiences to your card. What do you see in your outer life that relates to your personal Ace of Swords card? This may take some time. Maybe you wish to leave your Ace of Swords card out and write once a day, once a week, monthly, or use it in a time capsule sort of way where we you tuck it away for a while and take it back out in a year. It is up to you.

Carrie titled her Ace of Swords suit, Ace of Air. She lists the images in her key. You must look closely at the card to read the words she has included. Her Ace of Air poem key delves into those words, showing us again highs and lows of the suit— "I am the catalyst, the intuitive clarity, the soaring flights of the mind" and "I am also the too-quick judgments, the tempting certainty of knowledge." She bridges these two aspects of her Ace of Air with the lovely metaphor of the breath and its rhythms, drawing on images from the body and how our bodies work to bring her symbol to life for us in a very relatable way.

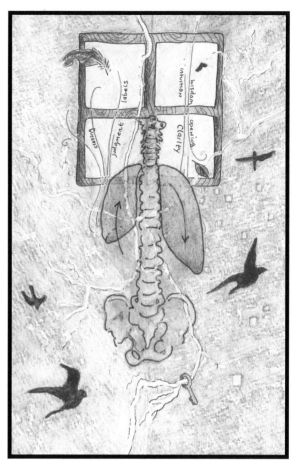

CARRIE'S ACE OF AIR CAPTION

The Ace of Air is the picture of a spine and lungs breathing, of a window, of the sky.

CARRIE'S ACE OF AIR INTERPRETATION OR KEY

here is where the lightning flash of insight occurs
simultaneous arcs and forking nerve impulses connecting space to earth
binding abstract to concrete
I am the catalyst, the intuitive clarity, the soaring flights of the mind
which must be taken in which must be inhaled deeply which nourish
I am the vertebra supporting the chakras, connecting the light and yet
I am also the too-quick judgements, the tempting certainty of knowledge
These waste products which must be pushed aside
which must be exhaled in forceful gusts to keep the dust from suffocating us
this is the wisdom of the breath

Ace of Dragonflies

LISA'S ACE OF AIR CAPTION AND KEY POEM

Ace of Dragonflies

dragonfly the ending of illusion
accepting enlightenment
flying true in the air

Lisa's cryptic poem serves as caption and key for her Ace of Swords, which she decided to label Ace of Dragonflies. She is anchoring the suit of air as dragonflies, so we will expect to see dragonflies on her Two through Ten of Air suit when she finishes her deck. When you choose to anchor your element in a particular way, it sets the premise for the rest of that suit. Lisa's interpretation for the dragonfly is powerful and to the point— "dragonfly the ending of illusion." The middle line of her poem extends an invitation, "accepting enlightenment." What bold statement could you give for the image you choose to anchor your Suit of Swords?

Tarot journaling questions to help you continue your search for symbols and personal card creation for the suit of Cups, Wands, Disks, and Swords from Two-Ten appear at the end of Section 2.

THE MAGICIAN

No sleight of hand, doves,
Just love's adept mirror
My cloak sheathed in yours

Oh Lucid dreamer
Soar off the easel of nighttime dreams
And into waking day

Who is the Magician? In the *Rider-Waite-Smith* deck, the Magician stands before her workbench with all four of her Aces at the ready. One hand is raised to the sky as if she is pulling down ideas out of the air, holding a divining wand aloft like a lightning rod. With the other hand, she focuses energy towards the earth where she will bring her idea or the harvest of her listening into manifestation.

Now that you have made your own Aces, go back and review them. Go ahead and lay them out in a row on the table. What would you call the Magician, the person who wields your Aces? Weaver? Storyteller? Hearthmaker? What personal magic do your Aces make possible? Let yourself play. For example, Caitlin Matthews of *The Celtic Wisdom Tarot* calls the Magician "The Decider" (25). Here are some other names for the Magician— Magus, Juggler, Aladdin, Mediator. Alejandro Jodorowsky and Marianne Costa in *The Way of Tarot: The Spiritual Teacher in the Cards* define the Magician as "an androgynous individual working with light and shadow, juggling from the unconscious to the superconscious" (127).

WORDS FOR THE MAGICIAN

Channeling, Divining, Wizarding, Transforming, Performing, Powering, Connecting, Juggling, Persuading, Cunning, Manipulating, Inspiring, Communicating, Intending, Influencing

MAGICIAN TAROT TIMELINE

Reflect and look for patterns in your past experiences of yourself, other people, and the world in relation to the Magician card. If you haven't done so already, set your Magician card out in your chosen spot. Take out your journal and unfurl the butcher paper roll for your Tarot Timeline. Place your hands over your heart. Close your eyes and take a few deep breaths, allowing the heat from your hands to warm your chest. When you are ready, open your eyes and gaze at the card in front of you. Notice which portions of the card attract or repel you. Describe what you see. List the colors, objects, and figures; take note of the setting and landscape (mountains? desert? ocean?), the plants or animals, and the dwellings.

What did you first think about when you looked at the card? Did you notice any physical reaction to the card? Close your eyes and do an internal body scan. Answer all or some of the questions below, adding any of your own. Scan your past for times you felt powerfully creative or magical in some way.

How have you used the tools in your environment to work seeming magic on behalf of yourself or others, to create transformation or initiate a project or cycle?

Through what channels has insight or illumination come to you—perhaps even in this process of creating your personal tarot cards?

Alternately, consider the first time you ever witnessed or encountered someone you considered to be a Magician, either in real life or in a favorite movie or play. Write about that first experience and what worried, enchanted or delighted you.

If you've uncovered obstacles in relation to your Magician self, consider what attitudes or ideas you might have encountered in the past about Magic or Manifesting. Who or what has kept you from climbing the ladder of the imagination to higher states? Or from descending to deeper dialogue with your unconscious, discovering the creative energy that arises from facing the shadow (see "Conversing with the Unconscious" on page 105)?

Another way to mine your experiences is to revisit the four Aces, or gifts, that are often depicted on the Magician's workbench. Where in your home or your mind do you keep the tools you most love to use? Garden shed? Garage? Study? A spare room housing your sewing machine, weight-training equipment, or paints? The Aces, our birthright elements, are the tools the Magician keeps on her workbench. They signify her fluid and dynamic way of playing in the world to create beauty and inspiration. She also creates practical beauty, so don't overlook what you naturally bring to the table. Look over your tarot journal and re-read your entries about your Aces. Consider your Tarot Timeline as you prepare to engage with the Magician.

PLOT YOUR MEMORIES OF PAST MAGICIAN JOURNEYS ON YOUR TAROT TIMELINE

Put in the date and select just a few key phrases to jog your memory for when you look back at your timeline in the future. *When in the past did you create a magical experience for yourself or others?*

HUNT FOR TREASURE IN YOUR HOME

Look for anything that relates to the Magician. Gather up items to place around your Magician card. What books, art, or objects remind you of the world of magic? Of a person who creates a sense of magic for others? Does anything in your home suggest the idea of combining resources to create something new from disparate elements (especially water, fire, earth, air)? Take a photograph of your Magician treasures and print it out for your journal. Reflect on each item— *I chose the following items for my Magician treasure hunt because…*

TREASURE HUNT OR OMEN-HUNT IN THE OUTER WORLD

As you go about your day, look for anything that reminds you of the Magician. Record in your journal the things you encounter. Can you find popular culture images for the Magician? Did you run into someone playing the Magician? A street juggler? A barrista making a masterpiece of foam to top your coffee? Consider movie characters and/or comic books, or hunt among your children's books, your roommate's magazine stash. At the end of your day (or week, or month), journal to the statement— *I witnessed the following expressions of the Magician card this week.*

PERSONAL TAROT CARD CREATION: DAYDREAMING, DRAFTING, SKETCHING, DOODLING—"ARTING"

Revisit the Aces again as you practice your vision, imagine what you'd like to call in, create, or invite of your dreams and desires—

Ace of Cups— *What emotions or gifts of the heart do you wish to offer or call upon as you go forward?*

Ace of Wands— *How can you ignite your most authentic, creative, passionately alive self? How can you ignite the same in others?*

Ace of Disks— *What sort of hearth, wealth, health, or connection with nature do you wish for yourself and others?*

Ace of Swords— *Where do you wish to point the arrow of your thoughts, intuition, and mental focus, and towards what end?*

Revisit your notes about naming your Magician, or delve in again. If you haven't already, define what magic, manifestation, and mystery mean to you. And then, when you are ready, move into journaling to the following questions—

What magic is afoot deep within your heart?

What would you love to call forth fearlessly for yourself and others?

Where are you being called to create beauty, magic, and joy in your life or in the lives of others?

How can you use the resources you presently have in your life—your hands, heart, mind, and passion—to transform, enchant, and uplift?

Step right into doodle/art/drawing/play.

Address in a freewrite— *"Dear Dream Magician, I would like to create a synergy between the following gifts in order to create..."*

STAYING CONNECTED TO YOUR PERSONAL MAGICIAN CARD

Set your card out where you can see and enjoy it. What do you see in your outer life that relates to your personal Magician card? Continue to journal, giving yourself plenty of time to work with your newly created card.

Carrie chose the image of a raven for her Magician card. Notice how she incorporates symbols from her prior Aces, and that she also references them in her poetry key, "I am the internal witnesses, salves, ladders, handfuls of keys, and algorithms kept at the ready." She invites further mystery, likening the raven to a riddle, wayward and contrary, "I am a koan / an almost accidental guide leading to truths you nearly know."

CARRIE'S MAGICIAN CAPTION

The Magician is the picture of the raven, the mystic amulets the bird has collected, and its spinning manifestations on the external world.

CARRIE'S MAGICIAN INTERPRETATION OR KEY

wayward and contrary, I am a koan
an almost accidental guide leading to truths you nearly know
capriciously weaving spirit and intention into tangible enactment
I am even that which fills the negative space
I am the internal witnesses, salves, ladders, handfuls of keys, and algorithms kept at the ready
I am a metaphor in which the whole is worth more than the sum of its parts
and also a primal knower
carving intuition onto stones stacked as signs
so that others may know the way

Gillian's Magician card takes the form of a candle, lit, its flame flowing in rivulets of wax over its lip and down the sides. But as we look at it longer, we see the beautiful greens, purple, and grey forming the base of the candle, like mountain ridges or tree roots. What do you see in this image? Gillian sees a figure as well, as you'll find in her musings below. Her Magician image invites us to take the next step— "What do I do now?" while celebrating simply being present— "Here I am." It gives off light while the melting wax creates a spectacular beauty of its own, building up the base.

GILLIAN'S MAGICIAN MUSINGS

There's a strange sense of a person standing there in acceptance, as if to say, "Look what I am made of, mountains forming and candle dissolving. Not that magical nor a moment of laughter, but a "What-do-I-do-now," "here-I-am," kind of a sense. There is a "The Little Prince" quality about it—the head is the flame, robes too big for him, arms down its sides.

Tarot Journaling Questions for Minor Arcana, People Cards, and Major Arcana

Now that you've completed six powerful cards and anchored your deck-making, you are ready to create the rest of your deck. This could easily take a lifetime, so be gentle with yourself and choose a pace of creation that works for you.

You'll find questions for the Minor Arcana, Major Arcana, and People cards here. These questions are meant to help you continue exploring symbols and creating tarot cards, using the process you used in the Six Card Deep Dive chapters to play with cards 2-10 in each suit. Here are the steps to follow—

Take out each card (in the deck you purchased for study) and engage with it first by following the Basic Method for Tarot Journaling on p. 25.

Use your "tarot eye" to treasure hunt both in your home and out in the world for examples during the period you are working with the card (day, week, or month).

Journal about the card in relation to your past, adding the most significant events to your Tarot Timeline.

Use the questions below to arrive at your personal symbol, meditation, or tarot card based on what you would next like to invite into your life.

Enjoy your artistic process and allow it to be fluid. Maybe you'll change the form or medium you use each time. Seek out a tarot buddy to share your deck-making process. Have fun!

The symbol seeking/tarot card creation questions below are framed around the concept of joy, and are based on images from nine decks in my tarot library— The *Rider-Waite-Smith Tarot Deck* (Rider, Waite, Smith), *Thoth Tarot Deck* (Crowley), *Motherpeace Tarot* (Vogel, Noble), *Daughters of the Moon* (Morgan), *Voyager* (Wanless), *Tarot Roots of Asia* (Klanpracher), *Inner Child Cards* (Lerner and Lerner), *Wild Unknown Tarot Deck* (Krans), *Counterculture* (Haigwood). But you can always create your own focus and questions for your cards. You might revisit the word lists for the Aces when you prepare to start tarot card creation.

MINOR ARCANA TAROT JOURNALING QUESTIONS

CUPS

TWO OF CUPS

What has been your experience of a happy marriage (experienced or witnessed in others)? When and how have you been met by an equal (lover or friend)? Through what pursuits do you find companionship of the heart, or peace within?

Symbol seeking/creation— How would you now like to be met by another? What image conveys a sense of contentment and a friendship or union between equals that is balanced and joyful? What image could you create to portray your version of a happy marriage, either between people or between polarities within your own psyche?

THREE OF CUPS

List the times of celebration with groups in which you've felt cherished and joyful.

Symbol seeking/creation— With whom and in which settings would you like to raise your cup, share creative or playful forces? What do you see yourself creating? What three figures might depict your personal muses?

FOUR OF CUPS

When and why did you refuse a cup, an offering, either out of self-preservation or confusion? Did greed ever play a role in your past (your own greed, or that of another)? Did heartbreak or despair cause you to lose hope? Did any places in nature give you shelter or provide comfort during times you needed to be alone?

Symbol seeking/creation— What do you wish to have offered to you now? What specifically is in that cup? What image can you create of a sanctuary for times when life disappoints or saddens you?

FIVE OF CUPS

When were you consumed by grief, anger, or regret? How did you find your way back "home"? What emotional storms do you try to avoid (anger, grief, shame, disappointment)?

Symbol seeking/creation— What symbol can you create that represents hope and trust for you through life's griefs, regrets, and disappointments? What image can you create that reminds you that confusion, emotional storms, and feelings of vulnerability pass?

Six of Cups

When have you experienced ecstasy or personal bliss? In your childhood were you heart-connected to a sibling? Did a playmate's kindness and love take you by surprise or heal you? When, where, and by whom were the roots of your childhood watered?

Symbol seeking/creation— What offer of love might you make to a friend? What offer might you accept? What does that offer look like? What image expresses your happy childhood self?

Seven of Cups

What fantasies, obsessions, or illusions have you entertained throughout your life? What emotional patterns have you returned to that don't serve you? Have jealousy or fear ever dictated your choices in the past?

Symbol seeking/creation— Which fantasies still have a hold on your heart? What would it look like to realize one of them? What image could you create to heal a past jealousy or fear (consider the seven chakras or colors in rainbows)? What image could help your heart move forward in joy?

Eight of Cups

When did you decide, despite love and emotional support in an existing situation, to leave security and safety behind for new adventures? List eight fulfilling aspects of what you had at the time and why you journeyed on or chose to withdraw. When in the past have you experienced emotional shut-down or exhaustion due to over-giving?

Symbol seeking/creation— What image captures your desire to grow by moving on alone? What do you wish to learn alone? Make a list of relationships and consider the emotional energy exchanged in each. How can you take care of your own emotional state?

Nine of Cups

When have your wishes come true? When have you experienced deep compassion for yourself and others? In what settings have you found encouragement to turn within to understand what makes you happy? Where have you spent time rejuvenating?

Symbol seeking/creation— List at least nine of your unrealized wishes. What image best conveys your most pressing wish?

Ten of Cups

When was your heart bursting with joy and excitement? How have you honored the element of water and the rivers of life in community? What have been your peak experiences of happiness, love, and emotional security?

Symbol seeking/creation— What is your dream for total fulfillment of your heart, in relation to yourself, your lover, family, and community? What is your image for radiant heart joy and fulfillment? How can you honor the element of water?

WANDS

TWO OF WANDS

When did you hold the world in your hands, take stock and choose your next direction? What horizon beckoned to you then? Have you ever followed your intuition into action? Have you ever used your hands for healing?

Symbol seeking/creation— What horizon beckons now? What image reminds you of all you have accomplished and encourages you to leap forward from that foundation? What image depicts your crossroads?

THREE OF WANDS

When have you waited for the means to create what you wanted? When have you waited for your ship to come in? Were you ever able to combine three passions into something new? When has a sense of loyalty characterized your situation with others? When have you directed compassion towards another?

Symbol seeking/creation— What three passions are at present blossoming for you? What is your ideal image for using your inner fire in a virtuous manner with others?

FOUR OF WANDS

When did you experience a happy foundation with family members aligned to create a happy home? What were you able to reach for during that time? What rites of passage were celebrated in your life and what do you remember about them?

Symbol seeking/creation— What image conveys your idea of a home or foundation in which your creative or spiritual passions flourish? What image depicts the rites of passage you wish had been celebrated or would like to celebrate?

FIVE OF WANDS

When have you sparred passionately in a group of equals? What was the sparring about? What did you learn by standing up against the wills of the others? When has anger affected you, either by your holding it in or by your expressing it explosively, or directed against you by others?

Symbol seeking/creation— What image might convey how you can grow by being fairly challenged by others? What image might convey a battle you wage inside yourself, and what are the stakes of that battle? What are you fighting for? How can you blossom?

SIX OF WANDS

When did you win and experience being celebrated by fellow competitors or companions? When did you feel especially confident and radiant?

Symbol seeking/creation— What image conveys your victorious self, trusting and playful? How could you strengthen your connection to your personal fire and charisma?

SEVEN OF WANDS

When did you have to fight for your position against a number of opponents? How did you defend yourself?

Symbol seeking/creation— What image conveys your personal armor? Your willingness to speak up and act on behalf of yourself? What is your image for "staying on top" with integrity?

EIGHT OF WANDS

When have you been at the center of diverse passionate ideas for direction (home or world, public or personal), either from within or from others? How have you responded to a sudden change or news? What did you gain and what did you lose?

Symbol seeking/creation— What image conveys the way you wish to approach a sudden change of heart and mind (both your own, and those of others)? How can you stay open to new inspirations?

NINE OF WANDS

When did you use your energy and courage to protect yourself from dangers, real or imagined? What did you need protection from? Do you still need to scan the horizon for trouble, or is it just a habit?

Symbol seeking/creation— Which image portrays your inner sentry? What are you committed to protecting? What image might convey the self that has learned from past entanglements and can direct will, attention, and focus into new projects? What image conveys internal security, a hearth of the heart, regardless of where you wander or live?

TEN OF WANDS

When were you asked to be the responsible one? Asked to carry it all? Have you experienced growth in a supported environment or a community of cooperation? When have you expressed your creativity in a dynamic and powerful way, or created a peak experience for yourself and others?

Symbol seeking/creation— What image might convey your ability to stop habitually carrying it all? Your ability to not burn out? How might you release pent up emotion? What image expresses how you might connect more deeply to your life-force to create peak experiences of expression and connection? How can you honor the element of fire?

Disks

Two of Disks

When were you juggling multiple demands? Balancing inner growth and outer change? For example, did you keep your job and your body balanced, or your family life and your projects?

Symbol seeking/creation— What image conveys your ability to balance two roles or projects? What image conveys your ability to draw on inner guidance while making decisions about how to move forward?

Three of Disks

When have you found others of like mind to collaborate or create harmony in your workplace or home?

Symbol seeking/creation— What image best conveys your most productive and harmonious habits in support of your physical life? Which three people in your life could you draw on to guide your plans? Which combination of your ideas might create the most harmony?

Four of Disks

When did you feel secure about your investments in your health, your job, your environment, and your home? How did you create a balance between saving and spending (both your money and your energy)?

Symbol seeking/creation— What image conveys your home, sanctuary, sense of health, sense of security?

Five of Disks

When did you experience a financial setback, or fear of a financial setback? When in your life have you worried about not having enough, felt disconnected from inner strength or lived from a poverty mentality? What readjustments or changes came as a result of that hardship?

Symbol seeking/creation— What image could you create that would help remind you of your connection to source even during challenging financial or physical times? What physical activity best calms you doing times of worry?

Six of Disks

When did you attain success, when has your inner desire been mirrored by tangible external results? When in your life have you had to ask to be compensated fairly? When in your life did you have to distribute money fairly?

Symbol seeking/creation— What image could you create to indicate a fair exchange of goods or projects between equals? What image could help you explore your relationship to money from a place of confidence and security?

SEVEN OF DISKS

When did you work for gains that took a while to arrive? What seeds did you plant? How did you lose or keep faith that the harvest would come?

Symbol seeking/creation— What image or symbol would help you remember to trust that projects take time, that effort is part of the process? What image conveys peacefully sheltering work until it is ready to be shared? Conveys a shift from fear of failure to inner and outer prosperity?

EIGHT OF DISKS

When have you learned a skill as an apprentice? What did you learn through repetition, working under someone else's wing? What was the value or lesson in waiting to step out on your own?

Symbol seeking/creation— What is your "workbench"? Who are your mentors? What image conveys your willingness to learn from a mentor in your field? What image shows the possible benefits of apprenticeship?

NINE OF DISKS

When did you experience abundance and health, pursue leisurely activities just for the joy of it?

Symbol seeking/creation— Which image or symbol conveys your ability to enjoy the gains from hard work? Do you have a dream setting in which you enjoy your health and wealth? Where are you standing, what are you doing, and what are you feeling?

TEN OF DISKS

When have you inherited or lived in a prosperous family setting? When did you celebrate community abundance and harvest?

Symbol seeking/creation— What does family and generational richness and wealth mean to you? What setting and image conveys the culmination of living and working in a way that benefits you and others? How can you honor the element of earth?

Swords

Two of Swords

When have you closed your eyes to the emotional waters in order to gain clarity and get to the truth of a matter? What did you learn in that time of quiet? How can you connect to your intuition and third eye?

Symbol seeking/creation— What image best conveys how you gain equilibrium to make clear and rational choices between two options? How do you balance thought and emotion?

Three of Swords

Have you ever experienced the conflict of a relationship triangle? What thoughts—real or imaginary—flood you with adrenaline? What was the nature of your family triangle— mother, father, child? When in the past have you used group focus to accomplish something?

Symbol seeking/creation— What image conveys how you'd like to handle betrayal or failure? What image shows your approach to regaining focus when under siege from negative thoughts? Who do you picture as the best idea people you could collaborate with to create something new?

Four of Swords

When have you called a truce to re-align or retreat? How have you used logic to balance emotions when making decisions?

Symbol seeking/creation— What image shows the structure/retreat/place that supports your mental power and ability to see clearly?

Five of Swords

When did you win a conflict or argument and make off with the reward? Who was affected by your actions? When did you fear being stung by a situation or interaction? When have your own thoughts caused you to panic?

Symbol seeking/creation— What image best conveys how you'd like to deal with mental conflict fairly, defending yourself and meeting the challenge with the appropriate amount of pushback? What image can defuse your fears of being harmed by others?

Six of Swords

When have you left one shore for another? Were you the ferried or the ferryman? Who or what helped you with that transition? How have you resisted manipulation by others in the past?

Symbol seeking/creation— What image conveys how you can use your mind to stay focused and peaceful, aware of what no longer serves you and impervious to manipulation? What image can you use to represent safe passage for yourself and your loved ones?

When have you indulged in secretive, sneaky thinking and planning to get what you wanted? What was the cost of not confronting or speaking up directly? What tools have you used to focus your mind in the past?

Symbol seeking/creation— How can you admit to yourself what you want and go for it in a direct manner? How can you deal with others in these situations? How can you best focus your mind for honest, clear results? Which spiritual practices or teachings might you explore to do this?

EIGHT OF SWORDS

When were you at a standstill, unable to see your way forward? What decision or choice were you trying to make, and what interfered with your ability to decide? What are the tools you had then that you didn't see?

Symbol seeking/creation— Make a list of personal strengths and skills. What image conveys your ability to tap into your inner wisdom without distraction? In what settings are you able to hear yourself think?

NINE OF SWORDS

When has your sleep been interrupted due to anxiety or worry? What were the worries? What was happening? When have you found yourself under intense scrutiny?

Symbol seeking/creation— What image conveys your ability to focus on one problem at a time? What soothes you during times of anxiety? What is your sun sign astrologically—the image that conveys the strengths you were born to bring forward? What image conveys your ability to use your mind constructively, bringing the lantern of insight to your problems one at a time?

TEN OF SWORDS

When did a destructive relationship, job, situation, or way of thinking shatter your world? How did you regain perspective and make peace? Which thoughts, delusions, or ideas have caused you the most challenge and pain? How have you used words, teachings, ideas, or dreams—of others or your own—to heal or make peace?

Symbol seeking/creation— Which image shows your mind's ability to let go? What is the most positive image for your mind's fully realized strength? What image represents liberation from obsession? What image conveys the community you can draw on for support in times of great duress?

PEOPLE (COURT) CARDS TAROT JOURNALING QUESTIONS

People cards, or court cards, represent people in our lives, and can also speak of ourselves as we are in the world. Go through your family tree and your friends and see who you might match up with court cards. These cards can also represent your "inner family," that you can converse with in writing.

People cards correlate astrologically—Swords, Air signs; Cups, Water signs; Wands, Fire signs; Disks, Earth signs. You can also break them into four types, by suit—masculine alpha (King), feminine alpha (Queen), junior masculine alpha (knight), and junior feminine alpha (page). And you can think of these selves from "green" or young, to "seasoned" or mature. Below you'll find basic questions to use with basic descriptions for each of the "families" of court cards.

BASIC QUESTIONS FOR JOURNALING WITH PEOPLE CARDS

Use these universal questions for the people cards, along with what you learned in the "Basic Method for Tarot Journaling" section on p. 25— *Who might this person be in your life? What do they have to offer or teach you? How might they support you? If this card is a part of you, which qualities have you developed? Which might benefit you to explore? Dialogue directly with the card, "Dear King of Cups"…and ask your questions or explore your side of the relationship to either this part of your personality or this person in your life (some possibilities— journaling to invite a connection, heal a relationship, or working through a separation or need to disconnect from that individual).*

BASIC DESCRIPTIONS FOR PEOPLE CARDS

CUPS FAMILY: LOVERS, DREAMERS, SWIMMERS—THE HEARTS

KING OF CUPS

King of Hearts, intuitive, emotionally mature man aware of his heart and the hearts of others, at home in dreams, but knows how to navigate the waters without drowning in them; he has perspective.

QUEEN OF CUPS

She's deeply emotional, connected, and loving, sensitive to what others are feeling. She is a mature woman aware of who she loves and why. She can help others navigate the deep waters of heart and dreams.

Knight of Cups

Young, unspoiled, he rides forward offering the cup of his heart, and will fly to reach you if need be.

Page of Cups

She is willing to risk the heart to lead in a new direction.

Wands Family: Life-Lovers, Luminaries, Creatives—the Radiants

King of Wands

Lion-hearted, charismatic, might as well be wearing a fire crown. Knows how to ignite others to do his bidding. Acts, without holding back.

Queen of Wands

A woman aware of her past struggles to get where she is now, a sunflower heart, warm, with the ability to inspire others and ignite their passions because she understands how to use her life-force.

Knight of Wands

He's your alchemy kid, all fire and salamander cloak, plume helmet, eager and passionate. He'll even hold up the light to your past and help you burn off what is no longer needed.

Page of Wands

This little one is learning to speak up for herself; she holds the speaking staff, rides the updraft, has the tiger by the tail, fearless and ready to express.

Disks Family: Gardeners, Hearth-Makers, Entrepeneurs—the Earners

King of Disks

Knows where he's going and how to get there, at home, resting on deep security and financial foundation, eager to share his harvest with those he loves. Good community builder.

Queen of Disks

Like the Empress, self-nurturing, physically and financially secure and comfortable, able to care for others.

KNIGHT OF DISKS

Focuses clearly on specific goals, is confident and practical, hard-working, rides forward with a positive new investment.

PAGE OF DISKS

Confident in her body and her environment, determined, she is ready to start a new enterprise that could pan out financially.

SWORDS FAMILY: DECIDERS, EDITORS, SPEAKERS—THE THINKERS

KING OF SWORDS

Integrates head and heart, sees and speaks truth directly and clearly. Good sounding board for decisions. Counselor, editor, keen mind, knows how to clear up doubt and worry.

QUEEN OF SWORDS

The essence of clarity, integrity, and detachment, this queen discriminates truth from lie. Stern but still connected to child self (child at the crown). "Off with your fake head!" She will not tolerate deception, from herself or others. Knows how she wants to direct her mind.

KNIGHT OF SWORDS

Quick. Can be short-sighted and rash but has some degree of perspective. Willing to go back and revisit the past to help clear your mind of old patterns. Slashes with swift sword of thought, sometimes coming to the rescue, but may need to consider real world consequences and other people's feelings. He wants you to travel light and quickly like he does.

PAGE OF SWORDS

Full of ideas and ready to stir things up, she is vibrant and willing to do battle for her big ideas; her bright red boots signify her passion.

Major Arcana Tarot Journaling Questions

The Fool and Magician cards are covered in the Six Deep Dive chapters, and the Empress and Emperor are explored in the "Mother and Father through the Aces" section on p. 98. Here are some brief tarot journaling questions for you to consider as you explore the personal aspects of other Major Arcana energies, for use either in your writing or future personal tarot card creation. Use them in conjunction with the "Basic Method for Tarot Journaling" on p. 25.

II High Priestess

How do you connect to your inner guidance? Who or what might teach you to do so? Were any women in your family grounded and connected deeply to their spirituality or psychic abilities? Did any pass down an ancestor's stories? Were any the dream-weavers?

V Hierophant

Which traditional sources, intermediaries, or teachers gave you your understanding of spirituality? How did your father, other male ancestor, or other male mentor pass along traditional spiritual or religious teachings to you? What is your definition of spiritual source (higher power)?

VI Lovers

How do you love and whom? What parts of yourself do you love? What marriage of opposites might you benefit from accepting in your life? How do you love yourself, friends, family, lovers?

VII Chariot

How do you move in the world outside of your home? How does your career grow or advance? How do you take charge of your life? What is your metaphorical chariot made of, and what kind of armor best serves you?

VIII Strength

How do you connect to your inner and outer strength? What situations reveal things you did not know about yourself before? Which challenging situations resulted in strengthening you in some way? What are your strengths? What wild animals are you drawn to and why? Which particular animal might you draw on for strength?

IX HERMIT

How do you relate to the idea of retreat, sequestering, "hermiting?" Is this part of your rhythm? How do you restore inner equilibrium in order to raise the lamp of insight for others? How do you embrace aging?

X FORTUNE

What is your specific notion of Good Fortune, both within yourself and externally in your world? How will you know when it arrives? How do you count your blessings?

XI JUSTICE

How do you course-correct as you go through life? How do you adjust your compass in support of soul aligned action despite incoming opinions, thoughts, judgments, and events?

XII HANGED ONE

What do you need to learn from a time of stillness, waiting, or being blocked from progress? How can you let go, listen, and wait for the next step to unfold, even if you feel it is time to act?

XIII DEATH

What way of thinking or being has ended? How can you let go of relationships or situations that are no longer viable? What did each thing passing from your life teach you? What would you like to do next, in the regeneration that comes from releasing? What dancing can you do, free of old baggage?

XIV TEMPERANCE/ART

What parts of you are coming together in synergy and being forged into a higher state? What is being passed back and forth between the cups? What sword is being tempered by fire? How can your hands wield the energies of the creative cauldron? Who is your guardian angel?

XV DEVIL

What obsession has taken over your body, mind, heart, or soul? What structure have you bowed down to? Where have you used power unjustly or contributed to an unjust power structure? Where could you stop pushing to achieve? What is out of balance in your life? How can you laugh at your current situation, and be more present in the moment?

XVI TOWER

What can you no longer deny or unsee? What structure is coming down? What is being utterly transformed? How can you keep your eyes open during free-fall and rapid change? What are you feeling? What is your home "garden" where you can begin anew, barefoot and listening deeply to what needs to change?

XVII STAR

Who is your star self? Which constellations do you love and why? When have you experienced the cool, healing grace of starlight? How can you invite the universe to course through you? What star energies can you embody? Where in your life might you be a star?

XVIII MOON

What inner journey is calling? How can you become more receptive, reflective, and enter the moonlight inside? What is hidden in shadow or unconscious but calling to be revealed? What are your nighttime dreams reflecting to you about your waking life? Like the phases of the moon, what is waxing and waning for you?

XIX SUN

How can you step more fully into your unabashed joyful, dynamic, radiant solar self, giving off your particular sunlight? How can you be the sun at the center of your own life? Where can you shine, uninhibited?

XX AEON/JUDGMENT

What parts of yourself have been transformed by your acknowledgement, love and acceptance? What parts of yourself and others give you joy? What in yourself or others have you not forgiven yet? What can you invite out of the shadows into full light? Are you ready to begin again?

XXI UNIVERSE/WORLD

What cycle or journey have you completed? In what ways are you free and whole? Where in the universe do you truly belong?

Celebrate! You are exactly where you are supposed to be! Dance!

CREATING YOUR PERSONAL TAROT INTERPRETATIONS OR KEYS

Every tarot deck comes with a book or a mini booklet of suggested interpretations that shed light on the symbols, images, and patterns on each card. Because you've done the groundwork of writing about each card, delving backwards and forwards in time in order to create your card, your "keys" will likely write themselves for you. Below you'll find some options for how to structure your tarot interpretations or keys.

Focus on each of your created cards, one at a time. Since this deck is delightfully only for you (right now at least), you can be as informal in your tone as one friend talking to another. Or, for fun, try talking about your card as if you were telling a complete stranger about it. Here are some suggested ways to approach the making of your own "key." Try starting with "The Fool is..." or "The Ace of Cups is..." and touching on—

Body position/posture of central figure

Colors

Setting

Symbols

Phrases included in the image (if you included words on your card)

Explain your choices, particularly any symbols that appear and what they mean in your personal symbol world.

You might like to create your own interpretation sub-sections. *The Roots of Asia Tarot* uses the term "Divinatory Key" (Klanpracher 8) and *The Shadow of Oz Tarot* includes a subsection titled "Shadow Notes" (Cebrian and Masterson 9). Subsections might be useful, for example, if you decide to include interpretations of reversed cards.

ABBREVIATED KEY

You may wish to play with an abbreviated key, where you choose a list of five words, like the instruction booklet for the *Tarot de Euskalherria* (also known as the *Basque Country Tarot*). Here is the entry for the Ace of Disks—"Perfection. Achievements. Prosperity. Happiness. Artistic success. Opulence. Delight" (Erlanz de Guler and Cemillan 58).

AFFIRMATIONS

Or you may wish to develop your own affirmations for each card, as Angeles Arrien does in *The Tarot Handbook* for The Fool— "I am radiant. I am a living treasure. I deeply honor and value the unlimited resource of courage that is within me" (25). These could easily be culled from your journal writings or the Tarot Timeline notes you've already made for each card.

QUESTIONS

Or use questions to get at the challenge side of the card (a gentle way to approach reversed cards or blocks to the card) as Art Lande does here for the Ace of Coins in his *Art Tarot* deck— "Enact your life. Sense what you want to do and do it. Are you over-thinking, doubting, or fearing the lessons of failure?" (Lande and Wajczuk, 22)

SPEAK AS THE CARD

Speak as Jodorowsky and Costa do in *The Way of Tarot*. They do this for the Majors, but you could do it for any of the cards. They head each reverie, "And if the _____ Spoke." Here's an excerpt from the Fool—

"Did you know that transformation of consciousness is possible at any moment, that you can suddenly change the perception you have of yourself?... Stop being your own witness, stop observing yourself, be an actor in the pure state, an entity in action..." (125)

In this example, they use questions to address the listener. In other versions, Jodorowsky and Costa speak using "I," as in this example for the Strength Arcanum— "I was waiting for you. I am the beginning of a new cycle...I shall teach you to defeat fear..."(190)

WORLDS OF ASSOCIATION

And if you are drawn to pulling in other worlds of association, you could add your own list of correspondences for each card, like James Wanless. Here's what Wanless chose for his worlds of association for each tarot card in his *Voyager Tarot: Way of the Great Oracle* guidebook— Astrology, Alchemy, Time, Geomancy, Shamanism, Aura, Psychometry, and Chirognomy categories (52). You could choose any worlds you wish to explore in association with your personal symbol world and note what each represents for you.

PART III

TAROT EXERCISES AND LAYOUTS

Personal Cards and Full Deck

Now that you have written about your personal symbols and possibly created your own personal tarot cards, you have beautifully anchored your tarot exploration process.

Part III of this workbook offers you additional ways to keep working with the deck you purchased (your "home deck"). You could also use your own personal Fool card, your four Aces, your Magician card, and any of the other personal tarot cards that you created.

Dreamwork Meditation with Your Personal Tarot Cards

You've walked through your inner and outer worlds and have discovered your own symbols, the images that reflect your own life and dreams. You may have created your own personal tarot keys or interpretations booklet to explain your choices. If you have already written your keys, read them before you begin this meditation. If you haven't written your keys yet, this meditation might help you focus in on what you've chosen and why.

Place your finished tarot card before you. Spend several minutes simply appreciating your choice of color, symbols, the placement and posture of your central image and your setting. Do this either before meditation or before sleep. Consciously bring the image of your tarot card into your meditation or sleep dream field. See your card in as much detail as possible in your mind's eye, and keep it as your focus of meditation. Or invite your card into your dream field. Come up with a question you wish to ask the card.

Journal about your meditation experience and/or night-time dreams

You can also use the meditation to help you complete a particular card. Put your work in progress out on your altar and focus on your artistic efforts so far; ask to connect further with your images and symbols to complete the card. Listen to the insights you receive during meditation and your dreams. Record in your journal.

Major Arcana and People Cards in Popular Culture

In this fun exercise, you keep your eyes open for modern day representations of the Majors. If you've made your Fool and your Magician, for example, you can look for enriching alternate versions of them. With the remaining Majors in your deck, try this exercise— using movie stills or magazine pictures or photos, create a collage card of the Major. Or explore the court cards in your deck and look for living examples of the Queen of Cups (Queen of Hearts) or a King of Wands (Master Gardener, Artist). Write up a description of how each aspect of the image corresponds to the Major, taking into consideration the clothing, posture, and setting.

We are all, in a sense, the living tarot. You are the expert; convince us how and why this particular image is a representation of that particular Major.

EXAMPLE: THE MAGICIAN FROM *JOURNEYING THE SIXTIES, A COUNTERCULTURE TAROT*

William Cook Haigwood created a tarot deck using some of the extraordinary photographs he took as a journalist during the sixties in the United States. As he was digitizing his archive of images, he began to see the images as a historically relevant tapestry of the tarot energies. He chose Timothy Leary for his Magician, titling his chapter in the guidebook, *Journeying the Sixties, a Counterculture Tarot*, "Timothy Leary and the Ecstatic Epiphany of LSD." Haigwood described the Magician as having "a seeming alchemical wizardry, [who] seeks a truth that might free the spirit imprisoned in matter" (7). Haigwood goes on to write, "Magician Leary offered the Fool boomers their first Counterculture gift: a primary experience outside the self, masked as a thrill with the presumed power to germinate spiritual individuation and ecstatic understanding" (9). Haigwood points out the unforeseen consequences of LSD use and says that what "the Magician had not counted on was that his holy sacrament would be used to entertain instead of enlighten" (11).

Make Your Own Archetype Variation

Create a composite Major or name your own archetype based on a compelling image you come across. Write a definitive description explaining the image to someone learning how to read from your deck.

For deeper study of an expanded series of archetypes besides those we see represented by tarot, see the work of Carolyn Myss, author of *Sacred Contracts* and an 80-card Archetype deck which includes archetypes such as the Alchemist, Gambler, Clown, Advocate, and more. Alternately, for an in-depth look at four archetypes, see *The Four-Fold Way: Walking the Paths of the Warrior, Teacher, Healer and Visionary* by Angeles Arrien.

Honor an Ancestor Variation

Do any of your ancestors remind you of a particular Major Arcanum? Maybe your great-great grandmother read tea leaves (mine did!). Maybe your great uncle left Italy to come to the United States and became a sheriff (Justice) or struck it rich in the gold mines (Wheel of Fortune), or your great aunt became a famous recluse in the hills (Hermit). Reflect on the gifts of inheritance as you make your card and write up the description. Think outside of bloodline— ancestors by marriage (step-relatives) or even "claimed" ancestors (those who have become part of your family). You can always make more than one card for your ancestor. This is a beautiful way to honor your ancestors and celebrate the ways their legacy finds life in you.

Plotting Majors on Your Tarot Timeline: Face Up and Face Down

This is a more focused and intense variation of the daily one-card journaling practice. Use it to inspire future writing, introspection, or personal journaling. Remember to pace yourself with this kind of mining—working in this way is very deep work. Undertake it when you have time to process the insights, and you have a tarot partner, therapist, or other support. Try doing this exercise by selecting a particular age or time of your life (0-3, 7-12, etc.) that feels most comfortable to you, instead of going through your entire life in one sitting.

Version 1: Face Up Living the Tarot Timeline

Lay out all 22 Majors face up in a large circle or in a long line. Use a long piece of butcher paper as a base. Starting with birth, plot your major life experiences, choosing a corresponding Major Arcanum for each.

Or, if you are a writer working on a short story, novel, or poem, it can be very fruitful to do this for a character.

Once your physical timeline is assembled, either directly on that timeline or on another sheet of paper, see if you can travel lightly and quickly through the cards, using a couple of sentences for each card and weaving them into a narrative.

"During my Fool incarnation (or cycle or period), I was at _____ point in my life. I was seeking_____. My biggest challenge was _____ and my greatest joy was_____" (or make up your own frame questions).

You may decide to move around the circle in order, or you may be drawn to focus on how your story unfolds, selecting the Major that best represents the next aspect of your life. Don't worry if there are cards you do not feel a kinship with, or cards you do not feel you have "lived." You will undoubtedly be drawn to some more than others. You can also apply this kind of play to a Future Timeline where you invite in the energy of cards you love but may have not "lived" yet and would like to live in a deeper way.

Possible Organizing Narratives

1) From birth (Fool) to now (choose card). Or maybe even at birth you came into incarnation as The Magician, etc.

2) The story of one of the passages in life, starting with Fool card until where that adventure ended (choose the card that best represents the outcome of that adventure).

Version 2: Face Down Living the Tarot Timeline

Plot the significant events of your life (or a character's life) on your butcher paper timeline. Place the 22 Majors face down and select cards to represent the hidden dynamics behind each event. You may be surprised and enlightened!

Again, give yourself a couple of sentences to describe each card. You can also mine this kind of timeline to write longer journal entries.

Creating Your Own Introductory Layouts

Over time, the tarot becomes a friend with whom you have many conversations. You may enjoy creating your own layouts to address parts of your life that are asking for your attention. The layouts are another tool to help you explore questions, develop your personal guidance, and most importantly, strengthen your ability to trust yourself. Here are the steps to take followed by some simple 3-Card and 6-Card Draws to try—

Choose a focus—moving, career, love, a particular relationship causing stress, a behavior within yourself you want to understand. Or you can just ask to see "what I need to see today."

Take a moment to write a sentence about what you intend each card position to mean before you start, such as Card 1—show me the gifts inherent in path A, Card 2— show me the challenges I might encounter if I go down path A, and Card 3— show me an ally or steps I can take for the best outcome should I go down path A. Knowing specifically what you are asking before you turn each card over gives you the most clarity.

Follow the Heart's Compass method—shuffle your cards until they feel "ready" to you. Take a moment to place your hands over your heart, close your eyes, and allow the heat to rise into your palms as you consider your reading's focus. This moment helps you center, ground, and align. You may develop your own tarot blessing or prayer to say as you begin, or the touch of the hands to your heart may be enough for you. Fan your cards out and select from the deck or cut and draw as you please.

Journal as you encounter your cards if working alone. When you are working with a tarot buddy be sure to record your thoughts later.

You can also always pull additional cards, just talk to your deck— "Show me more about this card." Draw the additional card and see how it clarifies your question.

3-Card Draw: One Decision, New Job

Past— How is my past coming to bear on this decision to take this job?

Present— How can I best open to the possibilities this job offers?

Future— What might I encounter down the road with this job?

3-Card Draw: Two Jobs

Present— Me today, trying to make this decision

Card 2— How I can best thrive or what might present itself if I choose job 1?

Card 3— How can I best thrive or what might present itself if I choose job 2?

3-Card Draw: One Relationship Issue

Past— How is my past affecting my ability to (fill in the blank; i.e., have clear communication, understand) work with this person?

Present— Today, how I am currently relating to this other person in this situation?

Future, Next Step— What I can harness or address to resolve this relationship issue from my vantage point, or what I can expect to need to address?

6-Card Draw: Two Choices

As described above, you can look at two options together in this way—

Gifts in Path A, Challenges in Path A, Ally or Helper Card

Gifts in Path B, Challenges in Path B, Ally or Helper Card

As you work through your layout, spend some time tarot journaling to each card. Look for color, symbol, number, figure, landscape, and emotional texture patterns in the card, but also within you—what was evoked in you as you looked at each card? Pay close attention to your reactions.

Your emotional reactions hold the key to where the most "charge" is in the situation for you (no right or wrong here, emotions just "are," and they point you to your truth). Address what your underlying fears or secret desires are with love and compassion in order to allow yourself your full human range. If there are Aha! revelations, return again to look at the cards. What other narratives might be in the cards you chose? Or ask to see further and pull another card to address new questions emerging from your journaling. Always journal to ground your insights. I recommend working with a tarot buddy—it's truly amazing what two minds can discover together in the spirit of love, play, and growth.

Tarot for Teens: Using Tarot to Ask What Kind of Writer or Artist am I? or What Kind of [Fill in the Blank] Am I?

Tarot is a beautiful tool for teenagers, a way for them to dialogue with themselves or with other adults in their lives during their key years of discovering who they are (which of course is a lifelong process for all of us). You can also use this layout at any age. The idea is not only to journal to a basic set of questions about your creative identity, but to use the very same cards to inspire new creative projects.

Steps— Shuffle your cards and fan them out in front of you in an arc. Put your hands to your heart and close your eyes. Take a few deep breaths. When you are ready, run your hands over the cards until you feel the card "calling to you." You'll pull three cards, one each to stand for—

1) Who are you today and how can the cards encourage the expression of your [creator] self? (place this card in the middle)

2) What card can help you see something that is affecting your relationship to yourself as a writer/songwriter/artist/etc.? (card to the left)

3) What door is facing you on the horizon in terms of your creative work? (card to the right)

Look at your cards and journal to the questions above, noting the colors, images, emotional context, figures, and setting in the card using the "Basic Method for Tarot Journaling" (p. 25). Then, turn and use those same elements to seed new work.

Here are the cards my seventeen-year-old son pulled for this Teens and Tarot Layout (shared with his permission). We focused it around his identity as a musician and songwriter and I invited him to talk about the images that attracted him in each card. The conversation generated the creative prompts to arrive at his heart's desires. He chose a very gentle deck, *The Inner Child Cards* by Isha Lerner and Mark Lerner (illustrated by Christopher Guilfoil).

Card 1, Five of Wands: Who are you as a songwriter today?

My son pulled the *Inner Child* Five of Wands with an image of a fairy, Flora (see the five-petaled flower in the card above). I also showed him the *Rider-Waite-Smith* Five of Wands, which shows five youths standing in a circle jousting with long staffs. I asked my son what he thought the five sparring musical passions were in his heart at present. He said the many types of music he loves equally are vying for his focus; there are many ways he's feeling pulled to explore music.

Tarot journaling prompt

What are the five kinds of music calling the most to you and how can you develop them? What are your five outlets for music?

Songwriting idea— from the *Inner Child Cards* book, we took note of the suggestion to paint or color a mandala (Lerner and Lerner, 147). A song might include a focus on the five-pointed flower and the soul and the concept of dancing with the soul.

Card 2, Child of Hearts

What is this card telling you about how you are presently being affected by an energy from the past in relation to your songwriter self?

We looked at the peaceful innocence of the Child of Hearts holding open the shutters to see her flowers are blooming. His interpretation of the images led us to talk about how those flowers could stand for the songs blooming on the windowsill in the room. He saw the card as representing the safe and happy joy of childhood.

Tarot journaling prompt

How can you stay connected to knowing where you come from, and stay connected to the things that made you truly happy in childhood as you become a musician and bring your songs out of the bedroom and out into the world?

Songwriting idea— the simplicity of the flowers—celebrate that—don't overlook or forget the power of just appreciating their beauty.

What door on the horizon is waiting for you to walk through next?

We talked about the natural progression from childhood's innocent bedroom to growing up and entering the adult world. We noticed the way the knight is wearing armor, but his helmet, while it protects his head, leaves his eyes free to meet the eyes of others. He is sheltered but still receptive to connecting. The image suggests wearing armor while leaving the heart's door open as my son rides forward into the rest of life, offering up his songs as a way to connect to the hearts of others.

Tarot journaling prompt

How can you write songs that are not just about your heart and life, but about the hearts of other people and matter to others, too?

Songwriting ideas inspired by the *Inner Child Cards* guidebook— what does it mean to be a seeker of hearts, a warrior of universal love (238)? What does that look and sound like?

If you have worked with tarot layouts in the past, feel free to skip this introductory section and head to the Father Layout that begins on page 100.

In this exercise you will use the Aces (either your personal Aces or the Aces from the tarot deck you purchased) to help you look at the lessons passed down by parental figures in the four suits. We journal about the archetypal father and mother cards (Emperor and Empress) before exploring personal father and mother relationships. The exercise concludes with an invitation to create a card to honor a parental figure or to honor the inner mother and inner father.

DEVELOPING INTUITION

As you play with the tarot and practice tarot journaling, you strengthen your ability to listen to your intuition in order to make choices. But if working from your intuition is still new, here are some simple suggestions—

Should I do the Father Layout or the Mother Layout? You could flip a coin— heads, Mother Layout. Tails, Father Layout. Let's say you get tails, but you react, "Oh, but I wanted to do the Mother Layout." Give yourself permission to do the Mother Layout by all means.

Or, you could pull a tarot card for each option. Home in on the card you most identify with—mother or father—and let the images "speak to you" or nudge you in one direction or another. You are always ultimately in the driver's seat.

Or you can simply close your eyes, put your hands to your heart, and listen to the answer that emerges.

DEFINING FATHER AND MOTHER

This layout focuses on the universal energy of Father and Mother but you can substitute stepmother, stepfather, uncle, or other person who actually raised and influenced you the most (since not all of us were raised by our birth mothers and fathers and some of us have lost parents or may never have met our parents).

CONSIDERING EMOTIONS

When trying the Mother and Father layouts, you are likely to come across pockets of emotions and memories you may have tucked away and forgotten about. Strong emotion may surface. This is a natural part of the process and actually a sign you are doing the work of healing, releasing energy from the past, and freeing more of yourself to be present in the life before you. For that reason, you may wish to consider working with a therapist (or a therapist in combination with a trusted tarot friend) for the layouts in this workbook.

CHOOSING A TIME FRAME

Point the arrow of inquiry by choosing a specific window of time in your life—an age that felt particularly challenging or rewarding (lessons learned when you were a child, a teen, a young adult, or the present). And, if you are a parent, you can also ask to see how you are passing lessons to your child.

CHOOSING YOUR ENGAGEMENT LEVEL

You can use the entire deck for any layout in this book. Alternately, you can divide your deck into three stacks— People cards, Minor Arcana cards, and Major Arcana cards. Separating the deck into three piles in this manner is something I learned from tarot sages Mary K. Greer, *Tarot for Yourself*, "Court Card Personality" Chapter (82), and Vicki Noble, *Rituals and Practices with the Motherpeace Tarot*, "Fate and Personal Will" Chapter (21); only here we separate the deck to give three levels for working with the mother and father layouts.

1) Gentle introductory level in which you'll look at which aspects of personality were at play between you. Use only the people cards to draw from.

2) Gentle day-to-day life level in which you'll look at the way you interacted— use only the Minor Arcana—the ace through ten cards of each suit—to draw from.

3) More in-depth soul-focused lens— use only the Major Arcana cards.

4) Holistic overview level— if you are comfortable using the entire deck, use the full deck.

Feel free to come up with your own questions and modify the layouts to fit your own symbols that you created for your Aces. In this workbook, for example, the Ace of Cups is presented as a lesson in love, but maybe for you it is a lesson in inspiration or joy. Use your personal Ace's focus to help you look into the child/parent relationship.

CHOOSING YOUR WORDS

The layout questions below ask you to consider how love was "given" or "received." But you can also choose different words or actions specific to you and your family history, and you can do multiple readings. Fill in the word and the date for each different focus.

For example—

How the parent *offered, withheld, blocked, manipulated, meant to give, was incapable of giving…*

How I *asked for, perceived, integrated, negotiated, dealt with, denied, absorbed…*

Direct the arrow of inquiry in your reading each time. Not all of us want to look at "how I received love;" maybe you want to phrase it, "how I expected love to come to me," or "how I longed to be loved." You hold the word power and the focus power. Take your time. There is no wrong or right way to do these readings. If choosing a verb from the word cloud feels unnecessary, use the wording provided below.

CARING FOR YOURSELF AFTER

Be sure to give yourself a good dose of compassion and love throughout this process—pick up that phone to call a friend or tarot buddy or therapist. This kind of work can bring up strong emotions, sensations in your body, and show up in your dreamlife at night. Consider the armchair help of books, such as *The Anatomy of the Spirit* by Medical Intuitive Carolyn Myss (see the bibliography for additional suggestions). Offer yourself other body-based self-care (hot bath, walk on the beach, yoga, exercise).

THE FATHER LAYOUT: ACE OF CUPS FOCUS

The Emperor is the "father" card in the deck, representing masculine energy. Using the Ace of Cups focus, you are asking about questions of love and emotional connection.

Place your Emperor card out in view. Begin by using the "Basic Method for Tarot Journaling" (p. 25) to freewrite about the Emperor, noting colors, symbols, emotional context, and cues of the deck in front of you.

Next, move from focusing on the tarot father in the deck to your personal father—

When you think about love and Father or the person who raised you in that role, what comes to mind? What transpired between you in terms of love and connection? What did you wish had transpired between you?

Now shuffle the pile of cards you have chosen, either at Level 1 (just the people cards), Level 2 (just the Minor Mentors), Level 3 (just the Majors), or Level 4 (the entire deck).

Either use the wording below, or use the verb cloud to select your own wording—

Card 1— *How did Father offer love to me?*

Card 2— *How did I receive Father love?*

Card 3— *How do I now unconsciously relate or behave in this relationship?*

Card 4— Choose one or more cards from the deck with all of the cards face up to represent an Ally or Allies to help your consciously make peace with the relationship. Allow yourself to be attracted to the card or cards you feel will most help you. *How are these cards helping me understand my next step in this relationship?*

Journal to the cards you pull. What do you see in the color and image combinations? Let yourself freewrite to each card you pull. What is the message you think the cards have for you? Leave your cards out in your home space and continue to journal to the cards, listening to your body, dreams, and insights.

Inner Tarot Father

Just as in the "Honor an Ancestor" chapter, you may wish to make a card to honor your actual father. You might also be drawn to making a tarot card for your inner Father, referencing your journal entry to create a collage or drawing or painting of the father energy you would have liked to receive and which you can invite through the making of this card of your inner Father. This exercise prepares you for the making of your own Emperor card.

Words for The Emperor

Fathering, Ruling, Ordering, Pioneering, Building, Facilitating, Motivating, Dominating, Steering, Confronting, Defending, Challenging, Possessing

Example: Jamie and Her Father

Jamie is a thriving writer and healer, a spiritual activist in her community, and a mother to three grown children. On the heels of a busy book tour for her national bestseller, Jamie finally found herself with time to devote to writing a personal memoir. Knowing that her private life would soon be brought into the public eye through her book, Jamie came to the tarot table ready to explore her relationship with her family. She chose the *Motherpeace* deck co-created by Karen Vogel and Vicki Noble, pictured below. (For a closer look at their deck maker's interpretations, see the corresponding guidebook, *Motherpeace: A Way to the Goddess Through Myth, Art and Tarot.*)

DECISION 1: WHICH LAYOUT?

Jamie's first decision was choosing her layout focus— Father? Or Mother? She pulled a tarot card to help her decide— the Three of Cups. Attracted to the lush green grass and the playfulness of the three figures in the image, Jamie realized the scene reminded her of early childhood when her birth father was in her life. Her guidance from this card was to work on the Father layout.

DECISION 2: WHICH FATHER?

After addressing the opening journaling questions (*When you think about love and Father or the person who raised you in that role, what comes to mind? What transpired between you in terms of love and connection? What did you wish had transpired between you?*), Jamie had a moment of doubt and thought she should consider all three Father figures— a grandfather, her stepfather, and her biological father. Jamie used muscle testing to choose and, within a couple of seconds, honed in on the biological Father, affirming her original intuition.

CARD 1: HOW JAMIE'S FATHER OFFERED LOVE

The Tower. We see the Goddess Kali sitting on top of a tower, lightning bolts in both hands. Early separation from Jamie's biological father, due to circumstances beyond her control, destroyed the tower of her home from her point of view. Re-examining things she didn't understand as a child had opened her eyes to the way that early shake-up of the family unit seeded patterns she was living as an adult. Truths that were withheld from her—for example, that her biological father had in fact tried to reach out to her over the years—had caused further shake-ups when they were revealed, breaking down the foundations she had put in place to withstand the initial loss. She had disconnected from him; learning he had tried to reach her caused her to reconnect emotionally. Throughout her life, Jamie had experienced serial "Tower" lightning-strikes about her biological father.

CARD 2: HOW JAMIE EXPERIENCED/RESPONDED TO HER FATHER'S LOVE

The Strength card in the *Motherpeace* desk shows us the Queen of the Fairies sitting on the green hills of Ireland while animal helpers, each with a unique gift, approach her. Jamie saw the Strength card as an accurate mirror for how she had to adapt to abandonment and make adult decisions as a child (for example, having to speak up in court to choose her stepfather over her biological father against her will). Jamie realized that her biological father's free-spirited wandering both attracted her to him and caused her sorrow because of the physical separation. It also helped ignite her imagination and set her on her own path of seeking. She saw also in the Strength card an acknowledgment of her evolution through emotional and spiritual challenges, the ways she learned how to connect with others, and her gifts as a writer, seeker, and the accomplished healer she is today.

CARD 3: UNCONSCIOUS ALLY CARD FOR RELATING TO/HEALING THE RELATIONSHIP WITH FATHER

For how she unconsciously works to heal her relationship with her father, Jamie pulled the Seven of Wands. We see a group of women in a loose circle, one speaking up for herself, another challenging her with power staff raised. Here we see Jamie's unconscious response to defend her position—she's comfortable with a certain amount of conflict. She's been challenged over the years by other family members as she sought out the layers of truth about her past. The card shows an unwavering dedication to face life with eyes open and to stand up for what she believes in. Sevens are connected to the Major Arcanum Chariot card, showing us that Jamie has learned to balance the will of her spirit with the logic of her mind and to take charge of her own life.

CONSCIOUS ALLY CARD/S: HELPER CARDS FOR HOW TO PROCEED WITH THE RELATIONSHIP

Picking cards upright from the deck, Jamie used a process of elimination—*No, not that one, not that one, not that one*—until eventually she had a "yes" pile of three cards she was attracted to that could represent conscious ways to heal the relationship with her father. Why not? Jamie can have as many allies as she needs, and so can you when you work with the cards! Choose the cards that align with your heart. You will know when you are "full;" it's a feeling, just like eating. Only we are giving spiritual, mental, and emotional sustenance to you through the cards instead of food.

Jamie kept the Star Card in her "yes" Ally card pile, the Judgment card, and the High Priestess. She almost put back the Star, wondering at first if it was too soft and dreamy— "Disney," she called it. But we sat a moment with the card which allowed Jamie to connect with her feelings, and tears came. After realizing this was in fact an aspect of her child self who was holding on to the fantasy of being her father's little girl, closely bonded, she decided to keep it out of love and respect for that younger self.

She also chose the Judgment card, a card she doesn't usually resonate with in more traditional decks (for example the *Rider-Waite-Smith* deck, with its image of an angel playing a trumpet over figures rising up out of the grave), but here in the *Motherpeace* deck, she was attracted to the rainbow light coming out of the central diamond of an Ankh, a symbol for the life force pouring from the heart over the earth.

The *Motherpeace* High Priestess card, more tribal than in other tarot deck versions (with its image of a Ngere woman sitting between two pillars covered in abstract drawings), spoke to Jamie about the potential to come from a place of internal guidance, knowing, and power. Jamie can hold onto the selves represented by all these cards as she moves forward in her life— the celestial healing embodied in the Star child, the life force and rainbow heart of Judgment, and the inner wisdom of the intuitive High Priestess.

THE EMPRESS

The Empress is the "Mother" card in the deck, representing the feminine energy. Begin by tarot journaling to the Empress, noting colors, symbols, emotional context, and cues of the deck in front of you. Next, move from focusing on the tarot Mother in the deck to your personal mother:

MOTHER LAYOUTS: ACE OF CUPS FOCUS: WATERS OF THE HEART, LOVE AND DREAMS

Before we begin to draw cards to the questions below, take some time to simply check in with yourself, in writing— *when you think about love and Mother, or the person who raised you in that role, what comes to mind? What transpired between you in terms of love and connection? What did you wish had transpired between you?*

Now shuffle the pile of cards you have chosen, either at level 1, 2, 3, or 4 from above.

Card 1— *How did Mother offer or not offer love to me?*

Card 2— *How did I receive Mother love?*

Card 3— *How do I now unconsciously relate or behave in this relationship?*

Card 4— Choose one or more cards from the deck with all of the cards face up to represent Ally or Allies to help consciously make peace with the relationship. Allow yourself to be attracted to the card or cards you feel will most help you— *how are these cards helping me understand my next step in this relationship?*

INNER TAROT MOTHER: EMPRESS

Just as in the "Honor an Ancestor Variation" section on p. 92, you may wish to make a card to honor your actual mother. Or make a tarot card for your inner Mother, referencing your journal to create a collage or drawing or painting of the mother energy you would have liked to receive and which you can invite and receive from your inner Mother. This exercise prepares you for the making of your own Empress tarot card.

WORDS FOR THE EMPRESS

Mothering, Birthing, Protecting, Nurturing, Attracting, Harmonizing, Seducing, Fulfilling, Giving, Unifying, Mirroring, Creating, Burgeoning

If you wish, follow the steps above to use the rest of the Aces to explore different aspects of the what was passed down to you through your relationships with Mother and Father—

Ace of Wands— passion, will, creativity, and power.

Ace of Disks— body, nature, money, and resources.

Ace of Swords— mind, intellect, ideas, vision, clarity.

FAMILY MEMBERS VARIATION

Fan out your tarot people cards upright to explore relationships with siblings or other family members. Use tarot journaling to explore which gifts and challenges each person brings to your life. For example, the Knight of Wands might remind you of your brother, a Leo born under the sign of fire who steps in with an open and loving heart whenever you need an ear and can't see your way to the next step. Or maybe the Princess of Swords reminds you of your sister, who eagerly steps in with a solution she hasn't thought all the way through (though you love her enthusiasm). For more information on the People cards, see the "People (Court) Cards Tarot Journaling Questions" chapter.

CONVERSING WITH THE UNCONSCIOUS: MESSAGES FROM THE SHADOW

Tarot gives us a beautiful way to dialogue with our unconscious. You have gently started this process by beginning to journal and connect your lived experiences to the Fool, the four Aces, and the Magician cards, and perhaps the Empress, Emperor if you have done the preceding exercises.

The next exercise, Messages from the Shadow, invites you to take a step further into that unconscious realm with an even more focused inquiry into the unconscious Shadow. We tend to associate the Shadow with negative parts of ourselves, the selves it can be hard to acknowledge—

the selfish part of us, the part of us that says cruel things when backed into a corner, whatever that part of us is that we don't want to see or talk about.

Let's take a heart's compass approach here—gently and kindly exploring our own shadows. Doing so with love, empathy, and compassion can yield unexpectedly joyful results— releasing the energy formerly used for hiding or blocking that part of us from our conscious awareness. We are free to make new choices and see life and ourselves in a more balanced and compassionate light.

How can we see what we don't know about? And why would we want to know what we don't know? Looking at some examples may help you decide if you want to do this layout. And, as is always the case, you get to decide how deeply you want to explore and who you'd like invite to work with you, such as a tarot friend or therapist.

Example: Amelia and Her Marriage

Let's take Amelia. She knew the most complex issue in her life—the place where unconscious forces might be at work—was her marriage.

Card 1: the Significator card

For the card revealing her relationship to this issue (her marriage) she pulled the Eight of Swords. In the *Rider-Waite-Smith* deck, we see a young woman standing bound and blindfolded, a bank of swords behind her, and in the far distance behind her, the roof of her home.

"Yes," Amelia said to her friend, "I feel completely immobilized. Tongue-tied. I should know what to do and I just don't."

CARD 2: A MESSAGE FROM HER SHADOW SELF

The card Amelia then pulled about her marriage represented what her Shadow wanted her to understand. She pulled The Tower card. In the *Rider-Waite-Smith* image, a bolt of lightning has toppled the top of the tower, and two figures are falling from the tower. Some previously shrouded truth has been brought to the surface and can no longer be unseen.

Amelia felt a deep sense of relief. She felt very much like one of those figures in free fall from a destroyed structure—in transition. What surprised her was that her partner was falling with her. She'd been unwilling to admit that things were falling apart or that her partner might be hurting, too. She had wanted the Tower of the marriage to remain in place.

CARD 3: A HELPER CARD

Next Amelia drew, the Page of Wands. A young woman holds a blossoming staff in her hands. She's learning to speak up for herself in the real, physical world. Talking with her tarot companion, Amelia realized that she hadn't been able to communicate at all in her marriage. She felt she could better face the wrecked Tower of her marriage knowing that she was going to have to stand on her own two feet again, barefoot in the garden. She decided she could try to call on this braver self who was willing to risk speaking up.

She decided to talk to her partner, even though she felt vulnerable, like the Page of Wands. She held on to the image showing that both people were falling, equally in transition. Looking at the red roof of the house behind the blindfolded figure, and the tiny salamanders on the yellow cloak of the Page of Wands, Amelia suddenly remembered her childhood love for hermit crabs. She hoped she could find the next new home that was just right for her, whether or not that included her partner. "A hermit crab," her tarot companion said, "usually only has room for one in their shell," and the two friends laughed.

Amelia hadn't wanted to see that her marriage was changing and had been clinging to the old structure at all costs. The tarot gave her a safe way to imagine herself into a scene and begin to picture what change might look like. The energy it had been taking to deny that things were falling apart returned, a tiny opening in her heart, a willingness to speak. A few deep breaths, some tears, and a little laughter about the hermit crab provided some stress release for her, as did the healing company of an empathic friend. There were definitely challenging conversations ahead of her and more work to be done, but the reading helped relieve some of her tension.

PREPARING TO START YOUR OWN LAYOUT

BE KIND TO YOURSELF

This is brave work. It makes sense if you feel resistant to looking at difficult situations and behaviors, for our shadows are the parts of ourselves we reject and judge. A whole range of emotions and reactions may well up inside of us. Maybe we want to deny what we said or thought or did. Maybe we feel ashamed. Or maybe we want to jump in and try to fix things that aren't truly our responsibility to carry. Feeling ashamed, having the urge to cry or run away, or wanting to laugh are all normal responses to this kind of work. Feelings of relief, empowerment, and excitement may arise too. The tarot gives us a safe way to look at a situation from any viewpoint we want to try on, and then another.

CHOOSE YOUR SUPPORT

You may wish to start with a tarot companion and simply journal about the situation for as long as you need before taking any action to address it. Or you may wish to connect with a therapist who can provide a safe space for these explorations.

CHOOSE YOUR LEVEL OF ENGAGEMENT

Divide your deck into three piles (Majors, Minors, People cards). Look over the three arcs of cards face up. Do you want to use the entire deck, as Amelia did? Or would you rather just use the daily cards (Minors)? Do you want to look at the situation entirely through a soul-lesson lens (Major Arcana)? Or to look solely at the personalities involved (People cards).

BEGIN

Hand to heart, close your eyes and focus on the issue for which you'd like to connect to your shadow's message. It's also okay to simply ask to connect to whatever you need to learn that day. Open your eyes and shuffle your tarot cards until they feel ready. Fan them out in an arc and pick three cards representing the three areas below.

CARD 1—SIGNIFICATOR

This is you today in relation to the issue weighing on you.

CARD 2—THE MESSAGE

What your shadow wants you to understand in relation.

CARD 3—THE HELPER OR BRIDGE CARD

What you can lean on for strength.

Discuss each of the cards with your tarot reader, tarot buddy, or therapist, or journal to each card using the method you've learned in this book, listing colors, objects, figures, and describing the mood of each card and how it relates to the situation you are observing in your life.

What one insight or idea can you work on understanding for the week? Is there an action you can commit to taking in relation to your newly gained insights? Be sure to pay attention to night-time dreams as well.

PART IV

TAROT-BASED ESSAYS, POETRY, AND ART EXERCISES

Tarot for Two

Do you have a friend you'd like to pair up with to study the tarot or to play with this workbook? You may decide to keep your journey private or share it with a few others, or, if you are a writer, you may decide to create your own blog or inspire other writing projects. Here is the introduction to Tarot for Two, the backstory of how the project began, followed by an example of the writing it engendered, and steps for you to take to begin your own Tarot for Two adventure.

Where to begin? But with a cup of tea, and a friend. And one's open heart, full of the secret questions and weights of the day. And a deck of images to consider in relation to those questions.

I met Mary in Iowa City at a potluck. Within fifteen minutes we moved on from the known (our love of words as writers), to our love of searching the unknown for answers, to how our minds and hearts worked. We both had tarot decks, we discovered, and though we came with other friends that day, we left with a fast date to meet and throw the tarot cards.

Over the course of the seven years I lived in the heartland, Mary and I played with the tarot cards through all manner of life changes—highs and lows—whether we traversed failed love, failed jobs, publishing successes, or life path changes, the joy remained steadfast for the chance to sit down together over a cup of tea (or once a year during the holidays, a quarter glass of sherry).

I experience a lovely rush of anticipation every time— what will the cards say to me today? Each card, face down, waits on the table between us to be turned over and revealed like a tiny messenger. Then there's the particular constellation of cards in relation to one another to consider, a collective riddle we approach with curiosity and levity tempered by respect for our lives and our vulnerabilities.

As is often the case in life, we found during tarot readings we tended to be hardest on ourselves. The mirror of Mary, a trusted friend for over twenty years now, has proved essential over the years, as I'll often project my worst fears or outcomes onto the images on the table. Mary will say things I never thought of, just as I will listen to her take on the particulars of her life and what the cards might be referring to and offer back to her the kinder, gentler interpretation I see emerging from my point of view.

Because we now live in separate regions of the country—Mary in Iowa and Tania in California— we do tarot long distance over the phone. At the end of our monthly tarot sessions we each pick a card to keep close by during the coming month, and the next time we meet we write about what the card had to do with the month we just went through.

Here's an example from a day in August, 2015, when Mary and I both pulled the same card— the Death card. I chose this entry because the Death card, naturally, inspires a fearful reaction in all of us, even for seasoned tarot readers as you'll find below in the essays about pulling the Death card. Have you ever mentioned the tarot and had someone say, "Oh, I'd never get a reading, what if I get the Death card?" When you fan out the majors, you'll notice the Death card falls in the middle of the trajectory, because, in actuality, we come up against losses over and over again in our lives. We are not meant to predict death or consider that the Death card means physical death for us or for the person we are reading for; instead we are asked to consider what is changing, falling away, what we are being asked to let go of or where we are clinging to a situation, person, or aspect of ourselves or our dreams or past. This is the kind of soul seeking the cards invite. Here's what Mary and I explored on the day it fell for both of us.

LOOKING AT DEATH WITH MARY

TANIA

Mary and I both pulled the Death card in August as our card of the month. That's never happened—pulling the same exact card—in the three years we've been on this project. And wouldn't you know, it's the juggernaut of tarot cards, the King of Kings, the arcanum Jodoroswky and Costa call, "the Nameless Arcanum" (199). Lady Frieda Harris, artist of the *Thoth* deck, paints Death with vibrancy—such gleeful fervor emanating from her dancing skeleton with his black scythe and black bucket helmet tilted askew.

In the card's background, I love the blues of the serpent and catfish with glum gold cat's eyes behind our "blue-eyed boy / Mr. Death" (cummings, 183) and the down-splayed bell of a flower stuck to pale earthen cave, scorpion tail curved in warning. Jodorowsky and Costa say the "skeleton of Arcanum XIII could be that of the Fool on an x-ray" (200), and I agree—the Fool minus flesh but still dancing.

Rachel Pollack reminds us that, "Death does not actually refer to transformation. Rather, it shows us the precise moment at which we give up the old masks and allow the transformation to take place" (*Seventy-Eight Degrees of Wisdom*, 102). As long-time tarot readers, Mary and I often reassure querents, "Oh, but the Death card doesn't have to signify one's death or the death of others." But when it falls for both of us, we don't buy that line either right away…and endure a bit of stunned silence.

We select ameliorating cards. I get the Ten of Wands and I stop there since it is an image of burnout, a reminder not to shoulder everything alone. Mary pulls a kinder card—the Prince of Cups, but she decides to forego writing about him since he's her second choice. We slip into child's play, addressing Mary's Prince of Cups card, placating him with apologies as if he'll somehow punish us if she doesn't write about him. We both know better and it is good to laugh. And it is a blessing to face Death with Mary. Years of sharing images and dreams have woven a hammock of kindness between us. I would visit her from the other side just as she would visit me; our work together would go on regardless of physical form but, for today, I'm grateful for the sound of her laughter on the other end of the line.

Honestly, in my life, the Death card does refer to the possibility of physical death given the illnesses of several members of my family. But so far everyone's alive and well. I thought maybe it referred to the reversal of menopause, a death I thought final with six months of freedom behind me until I went on a desert writing retreat with 120 women and promptly began to bleed.

So I, too, go down the path I tell querents to go down— *what in my life is dying metaphorically?* I know what is blooming— a sweet sense of peace I found at the *A Room of Her Own Foundation* retreat in New Mexico. I'm noticing the stars in a way I haven't for years, what with raising kids and the habitual fear of the dark and fear of men, spurred by a spate of sour lover stories and a date rape I was able to write down and begin to let go of in my first poetry book.

My casita at Ghost Ranch sat at the far end of a dusty road nestled at the foot of the mesas. Some nights I walked accompanied by sisters, reveling in learning what burgeoned to the surface in the heart of their desert mirror. But three nights near midnight, I walked alone from the fire ring where women sat sharing chocolate all the way over to the rooms in Corral Block by the ranch's entrance where women splayed across blankets to talk daughters, drink bourbon, wine, water, and watch the Perseid meteors fall.

The long unlit stretch of road was nearly unbearable, my fear eclipsed only for seconds at a time by the beauty of the blue tails left behind meteors streaking to extinction against the Milky Way. Passing the path that lead to the labyrinth, I took comfort in the knowledge of the spiral stone lined path—just its existence—quietly waiting for the next set of feet to enter.

The tiny sphere of my flashlight clipped to my sleeve lit my path one footfall at a time. No animal or man jumped out of the shadows to overtake me, only a classmate from my fairytale class emerging in a row of three halos of light advancing in laughter, a flash of shins. She reached out as we passed abreast to say, "Is that you? It's me! How about some Sambuca?"

By day, once, a blue-eyed man did step abruptly off the path to face me. But he was in tears, fresh from visiting the burial shrines of several of his friends. He asked if it was my first time at Ghost Ranch, spoke of his love for the land and went on his way.

Also by day, the shadow pain of raising my teenage daughter followed me into fairytale class. I ask, "Which fairytale am I living in? Who am I and who is my daughter?" The answer comes in a draft of a poem, *My Daughter, My Bluebeard* in which I learn that my daughter's body acts as a living key to the upstairs room where Bluebeard (men at large) has put all his dismembered wives (women at large). This is the old fear-based equation and the poem helps me see that this constant hyper-vigilant anxiety on my daughter's and my own behalf is neither sustainable nor desirable.

Perhaps the Death card refers to the death of this overpowered, terrified self. That moment when the masks drop and I get some power back. I am grateful for the desert's vast space and the women around me who held me psychically in our shared field of sleep. Then, bodily, *physically* during our inquiry with master teacher Diane Gilliam. She reminds us to go the distance in our work. *If you take the easy way out*, she says, her gentle voice filling the timeless dream space of our morning class, *you'll find waiting behind the door, the red shoes.* Yes, those shoes, the ones in which you can dance yourself and your pretty little red feet to death.

Gilliam also reminds us that helpers for the devastated always appear. Even in the Handless Maiden's Tale chapter of *Women Who Run with The Wolves*, the homeless, betrayed daughter without hands is met by a woman in white from the underworld. And in the garden, the pear tree lowers its branches so its fruit reaches the maiden's mouth (391).

Helpers, such as my sisters in the desert, and pear trees, surely exist in my future and my daughter's. Surely Death reaps with his scythe my fears— of the dark, of men, of what might befall my daughter…

…and Death finds me dancing as we did barefoot long into our last night at the retreat after the thunderstorm came and went, rain roiling the creek a silt rich brown, mesa cliffs crowned in brilliant white and blue dendritic tines of lightning.

MARY

Last month we both pulled the same card and it was a funny card to both pull— Death. First Tania pulled it as her card of the month and we laughed because it came up in her reading too— she's been getting Death a lot in the last year or so and, whenever it shows up, we laugh because we feel as if the cards are kind of taunting her in a friendly sort of way. When I pulled Death as my card of the month, too, we laughed even harder.

"But what if it means something scary?" I said, suddenly sober, thinking about the time I threw the cards with our mutual friend Tonya the day before 9/11 and we both got the Tower.

"Oh, I think the cards are just fooling with us a little," Tania said this time, and that made me relax again and feel better about getting Death as my card of the month than I would have otherwise. Death always makes me a little nervous even though it says in all the readings, and Tania always says, "It's not really about death, it's about letting go of something old you don't need any more!"

I figured that since the cards gave both Tania and me Death by way of playing a little joke on us, I probably wouldn't have much that related to it all month. But I was wrong. I've never had a card of the month that talked to me as much as Death did this past month. The whole month was like one big ending/cleansing/cleaning up of the past and there was some real death in it too.

My friend Rudy's father died, and the weekend before Rudy left for his parents' house to spend time with his father before he died, Rudy and I went on a little vacation to a place we loved when we went last fall. This time the campground with our cabin was noisy and smoky from a neighboring campfire and not much fun at all. That felt like a little death on top of the big death of Rudy's father.

The day after we got back, I drove to a client's house in Montezuma, Iowa, and sat in on a telephone conference between my client and a psychic medium. My client's dead son was there, talking to my client through the medium—my client's been talking to him regularly that way for a few years and I'm helping her write a book about it. This is why I was there; a few of my dead loved ones showed up for the reading too, my father and sister and my fiancé who committed suicide in the early 1990s, Jim Beaman. The thought of my father and sister made me cry but hearing from Jim Beaman—just a few little things passed on by the medium which might or might not have come from him—rekindled my sense of him, and I've felt him around me ever since. So, there we have the dead coming back to us.

This month I also refinanced and paid off some old credit card debt I've had hanging around for years, ever since I didn't sell my second book, which I'm now about to finish again. My book is much better than it used to be and almost ready to go back out and take its chances again in the world. Getting rid of the credit card debt felt like a huge cleansing and so did the de-cluttering vacation I took the week before last, where I went through all my clothes and my bathroom medicine cabinet and hallway closet and a desk upstairs and threw away a bunch of stuff.

I encountered many versions of myself during that de-cluttering, in old clothes I used to like but don't relate to anymore or no longer fit me, in the round self-conscious handwriting-of-the-past in old appointment books and on old checks, written to credit card companies I no longer owe money to, phone companies that don't exist anymore, et cetera. I found my partner-of-nine-years who's married to someone else now, Viktor, too, in the form of a manuscript of beautiful stately poems written by him about his old losses, the wife and baby killed in a car accident in the 1980s, the unhappy fourth marriage, the children who have grown up. I also found some poems written by me when I lived with Viktor, brimming with evidence of that life and that time and my old passionate love for him. I even found Jim Beaman in the form of a pair of dated wire-rimmed glasses and a deposit slip in his handwriting from July 1990.

I kept all of that stuff, but I threw mounds of old checks away, and I got rid of six fat garbage bags of clothes, a big cardboard boxful of board games Viktor brought to my house for his kids that nobody ever played with, and a bunch of other stuff. I carted it all to Goodwill, and when the guy took it out of my trunk and hauled it into the back of the store in a big cart I said to him, "I feel like I just took a big crap." He barely cracked a smile, but I laughed at my own joke.

To top it all off, when I went over to my shed in the middle of my de-cluttering week, I found something brown lying in the grass—a little pile of unidentifiable decomposing fur, a ribcage with a fat black fly buzzing next to it, and what might've been a rabbit's foot attached to the end of a jutting bone. I didn't know what to do about it and it's still sitting out there, slowly disintegrating, falling further and further to pieces, disappearing into the ground.

STARTING YOUR OWN TAROT FOR TWO ADVENTURE

Studying the tarot with a friend gives you the joy of time with your friend, the benefit of two sets of perspectives, and the gentle nudge of regular meetings. Use your own personal tarot cards for this exercise or choose one from the deck you purchased. Here are some pointers for starting a Tarot for Two adventure—

Set up a regular time when you and your friend can meet or make a phone or video chat date if you live in different locations. Agree on a set length of time to write to your tarot cards and your experience of the month. Then read your writing to one another. A supportive way to structure this is to make notes as the other person reads, on images and phrases you love, and then repeat them back to your friend.

Remember that tarot card study invites highly associative play. You are rummaging around and looking at parts of your life, thinking how they might relate to or embody the card of the month. As you begin to take your tarot eye out into the world in your daily life, you are exploring your relationship to yourself and coming to know more about you.

Explore tangential connections between the card and your life, for you are beginning to have a relationship with that card, and more importantly, with yourself. This is a practice of paying attention to yourself—your life, your associations, your choices, your body, and your interactions with others and with your environment. Sometimes it is difficult to pay attention to our bodies and our intuition; you may feel distant from yourself at first. But connection will come, and the joy is to begin, hand to heart. Start somewhere and know you are walking a labyrinth towards your deepest self, and every time you sit down you are practicing self-love. The journey is the gift.

TAROT AND POETRY

Both tarot and poetry use imagery to explore who we are and why we are here. As you've learned, the tarot's ancient system of imagery is used to formulate questions and divine answers about all aspects of life. It draws on images from nature, myths, and life scenarios to explore challenges and opportunities. The cards are meant to evoke not only external journeys, but inner ones—emotional, spiritual, and psychological. And its imagery has inspired poets from William Butler Yeats to Sylvia Plath to Kay Ryan.

In this section, you'll find exercises and examples of tarot haiku and other tarot-based poems, as well as a look at the *Poet Tarot Deck* by Two Sylvias Press.

TAROT HAIKU

Haiku create an exquisite, focused expression in just three short lines. When we read a good haiku, we enter the scene, inhabit it, and feel some kind of "Aha" moment of insight, realization, or emotional connection. The brevity of the form, juxtaposition of nature-based images, and pure observation create this sensation. The 5-7-5 syllable count that many of us learned is actually a translation issue perpetuated by early Western scholars, and contemporary English-language haiku poets often use fewer syllables, focusing instead on a seasonal reference, juxtaposition, and objectivity. But the constraint of 5-7-5 can help hone your haiku mind, so you may wish to use it for this exercise.

Writing tarot haiku forces us to focus on the essence of a card or the situation depicted in order to translate it into human, experiential terms. For this exercise, you may wish to start with a card you studied in this book (Fool, Magician, the Four Aces). Or select a card you'd like to understand better. Set the card out and journal before you begin. Choose your favorite lines from your tarot journaling or read over past entries and circle phrases to use. As you begin to arrange your lines, keeping in mind the confines of a five, seven, five syllable count, consider the following aspects of a haiku—

—A season (spring, fall, winter, summer)

—Juxtaposition of several images in nature or from human experience

—Pure observation (show vs. tell)

—Delivery of an experience conveying the emotional or psychological impact of the images and season on the speaker (in such a way that the reader can share the experience)

As you consider your tarot card, keep in mind the physical parameters of the card itself (a two dimensional square or round card containing a scene or set of images). Consider the ways tarot might cross over with haiku. You might address—

—A season, or emotional season such as the stage of life of the figure in the card

—Several specific images you see juxtaposed within the setting of the card

—The predicament or opportunity depicted and how the images and emotional season express that

See if you can bring your reader to experience a heightened awareness of a particular aspect of the card. You can ask questions in your haiku or write a series of haiku exploring more of the imagery or the imagined backstory of the tarot card. You can include spiritual, emotional, physical, and social dimensions. What storyline in your own life does the card tell? Let yourself play.

Here is a linked haiku I wrote—a poem that combines more than one haiku stanza—that explores the Wheel of Fortune, followed by haiku focused on the High Priestess, Death, and the Eight of Wands, by writer Tanya McDonald.

FORTUNE

Are you rim? Spokes? Hub?
Bearing apples? Infant? Queen?
Spinning for the spin.

Eye's iris, life-spoked
Heart print or fingertips
Soul's concentric home.

My fortune, my eyes
How I see shapes my bounty
Hazel ups and down.

(Pryputniewicz, Tania. *NILVX, A Book of Magic, II(II): Tarot Series II*. 2018, p. 43)

THREE HAIKU
by Tanya McDonald

The High Priestess—wisdom, stillness, mystical vision, Persephone
lockdown extended…
curtains open wide
to let in the moon

Death—change, loss, grief, ending, letting go
unfriending his ex…
the *thump* of a cardinal
against the window

Eight of Wands—action, speed, focus, go!
daylilies in bloom—
I sign up
for tango lessons

Suggested further reading (tanka): *Ink Dark Moon: Love Poems by Ono no Komachi and Izumi Shikibu, Women of the Ancient Court of Japan*, a book translated by Jane Hirshfield with Mariko Aratani.

POEMS BASED ON TAROT CARDS

Your tarot journal can be mined for lines and phrases to create poems based on the tarot as suggested in the Haiku chapter above. Circling favorite phrases in colored pencils is one fun option. Or write a poem about a card you haven't yet explored, using the tools you've learned in this book. Here are some poems to inspire you.

A FOOL'S JOURNEY
by ruth weiss (Arcanum 0)

one foot off the cliff
the other on solid rock
her heart in her mouth

night breaks into dawn
a fool sees stars in the day
red-twinkling in the sun

MA EARTH stop quaking
the fools are encircling you
with love returning

is this really dark
no moon & the milky way

in search for her word

she travels book in hand
the pages are blank

the dance of the flame
the picture in the embers
tells all ever known

down your beat wild wind
rocking to your tune all night
fool smiles into sleep

there - - - there the bridge is
every so often

layer by layer
she peels the onion she is
and laughs with her tears

(weiss, ruth. *a fool's journey: die reise des narren*. Translated by Peter and Eva Auterich. Edition Exil, 2012, p. 14)

HIGH PRIESTESS
by Rachel Pollack (Arcanum II)

Of what?
That's what she asked her mother
When she got the job, with
the pretty robe, the vermeil crown, the sharp moon
tucked under her feet, and
the neatly lettered scroll she can never
seem to open.
Of what?
But her mother was one of the Old Ladies,
and that's just the sort of thing
they never answer.

So now when they come,
the men in the fur hats,
or the long black dresses with
the high white collars,
she can only stare,
and look impressive,
and hope they don't expect
some blessing or curse or detailed instructions for
making candles or killing goats.

Sometimes she imagines she's somewhere else,
on a camel, traveling by pricks of light,
searching for a man whose name
is laughter waiting outside
his mother's tent—
or regurgitating webs from a swollen body—
or hanging from a hook
in her sister's meat locker
on the other side
of seven doors.

But she knows, unless
her mother of a thousand names
sends someone else
she will never leave this place,
the black and white columns,
the blue curtain, heavy
with palms and pomegranates,
hiding nothing but
a placid pool of water,
the tight scroll that tells her nothing,
and in her heart and in her face
no thunderspeak, no shining whisper,
only Silence,

(Pollack, Rachel. *Fortune's Lover: A Book of Tarot Poems*. A Midsummer Night's Press. 2009, p. 14)

QUEEN OF SWORDS
by Christine Stewart-Nuñez

Between geyser steam and glacial ice,
the newborn's cry and deceased's last breath;
between the ocean's moan and mountain's
whistle; between moonrock and lava,
between keening and calm, the wind blows.
Apply will and wit. Perceive with sharp
intellect the litter, dust, and dirt
swirling. In the distance, wind turbines
turn above fields. Observe and solve.

THE PRIESTESS
by Annie Finch (Arcanum II)

Heavy curtains close around my golden
Powers. But I wake in the dark noon
and seed quick shadows over the white embers
(I touch the pages). Patterns cascade down.
And the folds of my robe fall like water,
Floating candles swell with secret grain,
Long-hovering words begin to rain.
Even a book is simple in this folded
World. Though my throne is hidden, the horn-shaped moon
Glows where my foot has touched it. I remember
pillars opening to petals. (They are my own)
Such a quiet birth holds me. Earth's old daughter,
I keep my wisdom. I carry my own crown.

KALI—THE AWAKENER
by Marianela Medrano (Arcanum XVI)

I was standing at the threshold of becoming
your black breast poured a river of words to drown me in.

    You, Fearsome One,
        ripped up every layer of myself until I was no more.
We dreamed of the apocalypse before the births of gods.
Come, by all means, make me translucent,
        turn me into a veil once more. Wear me, burn me.
Let me be your tongue, your many arms, your three eyes.
Let me be the sword in one hand,
Let injustice be the severed head on the other.
We must be the terror we want to fight.
Your fury burst from Durga's forehead.
        Your body is the seed of our sisterhood.
Dark and naked, it holds us together.
Disheveled, our hair is every avenue to freedom.
        We are the eternal incarnation of fire, soul, and justice.
Let's catch demons with our tongues,
        swallow them, kill the others with a shriek.
        I see you there knotting the necklace of skulls,
        embroidering demon arms on our skirts.
Let's dance together to protect our children.
        We are the battlefield and the victory at once.

Poet Tanya Ko Hong writes about a deck from her homeland of Korea. The deck is called the *Hwa-tu*, a deck of 48 cards based on the twelve months.

GO-STOP
by Tanya Ko Hong

I was standing in a Korean Market line
I saw the *Hwa-tu* deck next to the register
I felt like I saw the little devil, the symbol of red
I hesitated to grab, but it had crazy glue
I paid and hid it in my purse and looked around to make sure that no one saw
When I came home, I hid them behind my books like I have secrets
I forgot about it like bad memories
I had a dream about my aunt, *komo*, who played those cards all the time
She snapped my hands, "No playing the cards"
They were taboo in our house, my dad lost so much money
Lost our beautiful house under the mountain
I wanted to move there when I grew up
Just one night, daddy played the "go stop" game and lost that house
That red deck is taboo to touch, it's got fire on it
But, I love to play finding fortune for that day, like my aunt
who did this every morning like she was praying to God
Seriously, after she played
she told us, "Come home right after school,
today there will be bad news,
what will be: do not talk with strangers."
She was the soothsayer
I played my fortune once in a while when my aunt wasn't there
My heart pumped
There were several cards that I wanted to get
from *B*, visitor, can be a lover
Also, letters: happy news, I want to have good news, a love letter maybe…

Cleaning my bookcase, the deck dropped on my foot
Magically, I sat down and played
I remembered all the rules to play
My fortune was bad news and good news, a drink and a visitor

So what to say, I have a visitor and I offer him a drink,
he says, I have good news and bad news
Which one do you want to hear?
Now I play this little red devil and make my own story

Two Sylvias Press created a tarot deck in 2014 based on famous poets; for example, Edgar Allan Poe represents the Devil (XV), Emily Dickinson is the Hermit (IX), and ee cummings is the Fool (0). Here's a sample chapter from their *Poet Tarot Guidebook: A Deck of Creative Exploration*, featuring the Queen of Muses (Cups) as represented by Gwendolyn Brooks (38).

QUEEN OF MUSES: GWENDOLYN BROOKS
handy angel in the sky

The highly respected poet, Gwendolyn Brooks, is the first African American to win the Pulitzer Prize (1950). When Brooks appears in your hand, she invites you to reflect on the caring, honest, gifted, and compassionate women who have inspired and encouraged your writing/art. Brooks not only mentored young poets, but she regularly visited prisons, hospitals, and rehab centers. She broke her contract with a large publishing house and thereafter only published her work through the small presses in black communities. In her poetry, Brooks empathized with the poor and the victims of racial intolerance. The Queen of Muses inspires you to be sensitive to and aware of the issues in your local community. Consider mentoring a younger poet / artist or volunteering your time in a school's literacy outreach. Maybe read poetry at a convalescent home or sign up as a volunteer in a program that teaches writing / art to challenged youth. Share your imagination, your love of art, and your creative gifts with those around you. Remember and honor the inspirational women in your life. Key phrases: pay forward the nurturing guidance you have received, have faith in the healing power of writing / art, support the ventures / businesses in your community.

Make Your Own Card to Honor a Poet

Exploring the rest of the Poet Tarot Deck can inspire your own "book of tarot poets," and the making of your own cards for your favorite poets can be a way to learn more about their lives and their creative and personal journeys.

Some years ago, I began a practice of using colored pencils to create tarot improvisations. I start by selecting three cards, either to address a situation or simply to help me focus on the day. With colored pencils I sketch out a drawing in response, picking up shapes or colors or patterns from the three cards to create a unique image that speaks to me. The resultant drawing is a synthesis of the tarot cards imbued with personal expression. It is also a way to play, or "converse through art," with the artist who designed the deck. I have always loved Lady Frieda Harris (the artist behind the *Thoth* deck) for her contribution to tarot art; here I got to engage in a dialogue of sorts with her as I ruminated on her choices of images and colors.

The example above is a drawing I made in April of 2020 when the Covid-19 pandemic was exploding globally and the state of California had just been placed on lockdown by Governor Gavin Newsom. I pulled three tarot cards that day, one from each portion of the *Thoth* deck.

CARD 1: THE MAJOR ARCANA, ART/TEMPERANCE CARD

Looking at the two figures in the *Thoth* Art card, I noticed the two-faced figure could be mistaken for a Lover's card. Here, housed in one body, I saw male and female halves joining, a unified lover of creativity within me.

CARD 2: THE COURT CARD, KNIGHT OF DISKS

Here the young knight rests a moment in his saddle, helmet tipped back, taking in the glow of the sun which is rising or setting on the horizon. I felt it was telling me to take this moment to slow down and let my emotions catch up to me.

CARD 3: THE MINOR ARCANA, TEN OF WANDS

This image reflected the state of collective worry (ten represents the culmination, or the whole community)—the fear of mortality, the human family across the globe suffering, from Wuhan to Italy, from New York City to California.

I opened my journal, took out my colored pencils, and allowed the imagery to take hold in my mind. I realized I needed to start exactly where I was in the moment, so I traced my hands, one with blue colored pencil and one red, in honor of the anima and animus I saw in the Art card. I looked again at the Knight of Disks, noticing that the sun in the sky was mirrored by an upraised metalwork sun on his shield. *Lay down your burden of fear, and rest. Learn to trust* were the words that floated through my mind. This led me to place a rainbow below the untouching hands, returning to the natural order of colors we see in the sky after a storm— red, orange, yellow, blue, green, indigo, violet. Like the two suns in the Knight's card (sky and shield), I drew a mirror rainbow, to indicate that while we cannot touch during the pandemic, we can create and share art with one another as a bridge of hope until the time when we can touch again. A journaling question came from the drawing— *What can I make with my hands to bridge distance between myself and someone I love? How can I heal myself with my hands, and how can what I make help others too?*

1) Think about the issue most pressing on your heart.

2) Draw three cards, one from the Majors, one from the Minors, and one from the People cards. Spend some time looking at the cards.

3) At the end of your meditation period (day, week, you decide), write about what you see each card saying to you about your issue. Try as much as possible to anchor your observations and reflections to specific images and colors in the card at hand.

4) Then take out a blank sheet of paper and draw or color or paint (using any medium you choose). Which of the elements in the cards speak to you? What image emerges that might inspire you to integrate parts of your life with joy, compassion, and self-love?

5) Keep the resultant artwork out in the coming days and weeks, as long as you wish. You can always create more than one response. Let it mirror back to you a sense of peace and joy; take pride in your work.

A Parting Word: A Writer's Journey Through Tarot Imagery

It is good to have an end to journey towards, but it is the journey that matters, in the end.
—Ursula K. Le Guin, *The Left Hand of Darkness*

The summer I graduated from college, I lived in the Sacramento Valley. That summer we had a record heat wave. Like every undergraduate, like any of us in transition, I wondered, *Where do I go from here?* In search of shade, I rode my bicycle through the olive groves. Tar and olive sap stuck to my tires while heat wrinkled the horizon. The sky suddenly filled with hundreds of butterflies. They fluttered in droves across four lanes of traffic on Interstate 80 and down the frontage road, wafting over my hair and shoulders, even between my tire spokes. I braked and stood, my path littered with pale yellow wings of cabbage whites. I filled my bike basket with the glittering wings of the perished, wondering what to make of the omen.

At that time, I had a hard time taking responsibility for my future or claiming a space of my own. Crisis plagued my love life. I meant to ask for a room of my own to write in but hadn't, yearned to write daily but wasn't. I staked out a corner of our bedroom, filling a basket with pinecones and driftwood from the mouth of the Russian River where I grew up, scattering the lifeless butterflies on top. I felt calmed by the wings—inert and grounded, just as I was.

Later that day, I found a deck of *Motherpeace* tarot cards tucked into the bookshelf. It was my lover's deck, abandoned. I kept it for my own, and from that day on the cards became my silent allies. With the cards, I turned inward to begin a lifelong journey to wholeness. Because there was no corresponding book of interpretations, I began by pulling a card every day and meditating on its possible meaning, just as I would have done with a dream remembered from the night. Eventually I found a temple nearby that offered a class on the tarot.

This was the 80s, when feminist decks had recently broken onto the tarot scene—not only the *Motherpeace* deck co-created by Karen Vogel and Vicki Noble, but also the *Daughters of the Moon* deck by Ffiona Morgan and many others. Daily I pulled cards with images from Kali to the Green Tarot of Ireland to kundalini-awakened girls spinning in wheels of fire. I reveled in the fertile range of traditionally suppressed images of female power. That summer of tarot and inner contemplation culminated in a decision to pursue my dream of becoming a writer. I applied to graduate school and was accepted into The Iowa Writers' Workshop. My tarot apprenticeship blossomed when I found a new teacher in the heartland, Quan Tracy Cherry.

As I fell headlong into the world of poetry, working and studying as a writer and teacher, I discovered I could also explore the tarot as muse. I began to correlate the tarot's image-based story line to Joseph Campbell's Hero's Journey and Carl Jung's work on the collective unconscious. Later, paging through Jung's *The Red Book*, I realized that tarot deck makers, like Jung, dove deeply into the unconscious to bring back images and ideas that still inspire art, psychology, and spiritual study.

But instead of relying solely on images discovered and put forth by others (and in the spirit of sitting in the seat of introspective power), I wrote this book to help you come to know yourself through the lens of tarot's fertile imagery and inspire you to take the leap to find your own symbols.

About seven years after collecting those inert butterflies as an undergraduate student in California, the butterfly image returned when a fellow poet read my cards. I was once again at a crossroads. My friend playfully asked me to choose an image to represent my writing life—anything—animal, plant—and she would improvise a reading, placing the cards in the corresponding shape. "Butterfly," I said, and she made a pattern of wings and thorax graced by a kite-tail "S" of descending cards.

The butterfly travelled around in my subconscious, flitting here and there, mostly forgotten. Another seven years passed in which I married a childhood friend and gave birth to our three children. One morning I walked out of the house to find a butterfly, still living, pinned on the windshield of our car. I wrote a poem in response. It became the title of my poetry collection, *November Butterfly* (Saddle Road Press, 2014) complete with initiating image of the inert butterfly—a metaphorical wing taking concrete form as a book and granting my life's dream of becoming a writer.

NOVEMBER BUTTERFLY

It's easy to love the sun
and the roses it fires,
blood cardinals
flying over snow,
three black horses
running midmorning
in the rain,
a blue heron
on a downed tree
in river's mist.

But what of tar fissures
on backroads off the grid,
a liver sheened reptile
clambering out of the ditch,
cold rims of hubcaps,
headlights, a voice
two states away on the radio,
a butterfly with a frayed
wing pinned living
to the windshield.

It's easy to love some women,
emanating green, moonskinned,
quiet, enchanting
as sunlight
through the undersides of leaves.
Winter in the thighs,
we hibernate in rooms they've left,
and pray they'll return, notice us,
or let fall
some butter from their palms.

I wish I were a flower,
or the maker,
to mend you.
I held out my finger—
not a stick—
and up you grappled,
unfurled a tunneled up
tongue,
for one last taste,
or to ward me off

So easy to muck the translation
no common language—
that gap between the self one loves
and the self one fears.
I can't fill out your wing,
but I can look you
in the unblinking amber screen
of your eye,

and set you on this leaf.

We all face challenges. We may not be able to change the particulars of what confronts us, but we can bring the self we love, the self we fear, and all the selves in between, to the present moment and begin to align with our dreams. As I say to every querent, "I am your tarot reader today. But the cards are yours." I am your tarot muse for the pages of this book, but the journey is yours. May it bring unending joy, peace, and appreciation of the gifts within you.

Tarot Blessings
Coronado, CA

July 2020

A Heart's Compass Note on Tarot and Fear, FAQs

Are you coming to this workbook curious, maybe intrigued, but fearful? Does the concept of taking guidance from a tarot reading—much less creating your own tarot cards!—make you feel uneasy? This chapter will help you decide if you are ready to begin a relationship with the cards.

Here are a few FAQs—

Do the cards in and of themselves hold power? Will my life be dictated and predicted by the cards?

If I get challenging cards, like the Death card, does it mean something bad will happen to me or someone I love? Am I somehow "stuck with that card?"

Will tarot card study displease my church, my spiritual advisor, my own internal sense of how I should connect with my spirit?

Do the cards in and of themselves hold power? Will my life be dictated and predicted by the cards?

The cards and their symbols' potency in relation to our inner work depends on our understanding of them. It is the intentional quality of looking at a situation together that brings greater agency and opportunity to discern choices. This happens through the conversation between reader and querent, a seeking of clarity that helps us see more deeply into ourselves and others. In my practice, before every reading, the first step is to place hands over the heart and commit to listening with heart-centered love, deeply and objectively, and to use the listening to anchor the intention to honor the highest and most joyful good. We could be reading rose petals or patterns in sand and we would always learn something about our minds, fears, heart, and soul yearnings as we converse about the patterns. Whether rose petals, patterns in sand, or an artist's picturing of human situations in the *Rider-Waite-Smith* deck, all simply give us a mirror to look into and speak about what we see. However, each deck bears carefully chosen symbols, patterns, and colors with years of history behind them, adding to their particular potency. There's much to be learned and gained by studying the specific intentions and choices of each deck maker.

We tend to see different aspects in each card depending on our moods. One day you might notice the bright red boots of the Fool and feel delighted by his plucky stance. The next day you might notice the cliff, and feel trepidation— why doesn't the Fool see that he's in danger? Why isn't she paying attention while moving forward? The questions that rise as you engage with the images help you see where you are in relation to life itself.

It is important to make sure you trust your tarot reader, feel they have grounded themselves in ethical spiritual study, and that they have your highest good in mind. Usually when we come for a reading, our hearts are vulnerable; often we are in crisis or we are struggling to understand our lives. It is a great honor and blessing to bring yourself, vulnerable and open, to a reader. Make sure your reader is worthy of that honor.

In this workbook, you are learning to read for yourself, meeting the cards one card at a time through a gentle and heart-centered lens of love. The idea is to tune into our heart center and navigate using our heart as a compass, to understand our questions. By listening to our thoughts that come up in relation to the images on the cards, we create an opportunity to see new solutions, new ways to move towards joy, our natural birthright. Often we are hardest on ourselves, so working with a friend as you go through this workbook can help you both hold your highest potential in loving-kindness as you begin to play with one, two, or three card draws. Then you have two hearts, two minds, two sets of eyes looking at your life (see "Tarot for Two").

If I get challenging cards, like the Death card, does it mean something bad will happen to me or someone I love? Am I somehow "stuck with that card?"

One of my friends often includes this opening prayer, "Make sure this reading is mine and not Tania's." And she's also famous for putting an entire reading back and saying, "These cards aren't really talking to me." So we do! We put them back, and she gets another reading. Why not? Should she punish herself or upset herself if she gets a reading that doesn't make her happy? No, absolutely not, for the first rule of the heart's compass approach to tarot reading is self-love and compassion. Often the alternative cards that are pulled have a similar message but told through different pictures, and we talk until we reach the root of the fears and gently steer ourselves towards joy.

If you are feeling fear still but still would like to begin to work with the tarot, here's a gentle way to begin. Instead of doing readings with the deck face down, turn the cards over and acquaint yourself with them by seeing them fanned out upright. Choose one card a day face up (see Basic Method for Tarot Journaling on p. 25). Usually when you draw for tarot readings, you are drawing cards face down, which can make you feel uncomfortably pinned if you get a challenging card. So for now, go ahead and pull a card from the deck face up so you are choosing an image that feels right for you. Once you come to know the full deck, you will find that you are no longer afraid of the challenging cards. In fact, on a day when you are facing a challenging situation you may just find solace in the card that mirrors how it feels. We always have agency to move forward; the irony is that sometimes we are stuck in the very state depicted in the card until we see it and can begin to imagine how to move forward. You can always keep talking to the deck. "Talk to me more about this situation," or "Let me now pull a card for how I can mend my heart in relation to this person, or grieve this loss," are just a few examples of countless ways you can converse with the deck. The cards provide an opportunity to conduct a beautiful, loving, lifelong conversation with yourself.

Will tarot card study displease my church, my spiritual advisor, my own internal sense of how I should connect with my spirit?

If you are concerned about card reading going against your church or spiritual practice, trust your heart. I don't recommend creating more stress for yourself by engaging unless you are ready. I believe, however, there is much love and joy to be found in creating your own symbol cards. In this book we are using the tarot's structure to help you empower yourself and find your own symbols. And we will pass through the tarot's landscape to do that. One option is to peruse tarot workbooks in the bookstore to get a feel for the many approaches of study, and you will find the one that is right for you when the time is right.

If you do decide to engage with the cards, here is a simple introductory tarot layout you can use to help you explore your relationship to spirituality, using the cards. Shuffle the cards and choose (from the cards, face down).

1) Spirituality as I was taught, how it was presented to me (pull one card for each teacher or phase of spiritual learning).

2) How I received it, or my reaction to each corresponding teacher or phase of spiritual learning.

3) Then select two bridge cards, one face-down for your unconscious relationship to spirituality. And one face up for how you would like to move forward with relating to your spirituality.

You can try this layout and point the focus of your reading towards any time period in your life, for example, focusing on what you were taught as a child, later as a teen, and doing a third layout for what you learned as an adult.

Tarot Blessings!

Tarot Resources and Bibliography

Image Permissions

Counterculture Tarot Deck. William Cook Haigwood, permission granted by William Cook Haigwood.

Inner Child Cards. Isha and Mark Lerner, illustrated by Christopher Guilfoil, permission granted by Isha Lerner.

Motherpeace Tarot Deck. (www.motherpeace.com). Co-created by Karen Vogel and Vicki Noble, permission granted by Karen Vogel and Vicki Noble.

Poet Tarot Deck. Two Sylvias Press, permission granted by Two Sylvias Press.

Rider-Waite-Smith Deck. Publisher Rider, Tarot Interpretations Waite, Illustrations Pamela Colman Smith (in public domain).

Unattributed art and short poems throughout including those at the beginning of the Deep Dive Chapters are by the author.

Tarot Resources and Bibliography

Allen, Mary. *The Rooms of Heaven.* Alfred A. Knopf, 1999.

Arrien, Angeles. *The Tarot Handbook: Practical Applications of Ancient Visual Symbols.* Arcus Publishing Company, 1987.

...*The Four-Fold Way: Walking the Paths of the Warrior, Teacher, Healer, and Visionary.* HarperOne, 1993.

Cameron, Julie. *The Artist's Way.* Tarcher Perigree, 2006.

Connolly, Eileen. *Tarot: A New Handbook for the Apprentice, Vol 1.* Newcastle Publishing Company, 1990.

Crispin, Jessa. *The Creative Tarot: A Modern Guide to An Inspired Life.* Touchstone, 2016.

Della, Jamie. *The Book of Spells: The Magick of Witchcraft.* Ten Speed Press, 2019.

Dickerman, Alexandra Collins. *Following Your Path: A Self-Discovery Adventure Journal Using*

Myths, Symbols And Images. New Dimensions, 1989.

Eliason, Mickey. *Reflecting on the Teaching of Angeles Arrien: From A to Z*. Create Space, 2016.

…The Shadow Knows Workbook: Uncovering and Integrating the Shadow. CreateSpace, 2018.

Erlanz de Guler, Maritxu. *Basque Country Tarot, Instruction Booklet*. Fournier, 1991.

Estes, Clarissa Pinkola. *Women Who Run with the Wolves: Myths and Stories of the Wild Woman Archetype*. Ballantine Books, 1992.

Giles, Cynthia. *The Tarot: History, Mystery and Lore*. Fireside Books, 1992.

Greer, Mary K. *Tarot for Yourself: a workbook for personal transformation*. Newcastle Publishing, 1984.

Haigwood, William Cook. *Journeying the Sixties: A Counterculture Tarot*. CreateSpace IPP, 2013.

Jodorowsky, Alejandro and Marianne Costa. *The Way of Tarot: The Spiritual Teacher in the Cards*. Destiny Books, 2004.

Jung, C.G. *The Red Book: Liber Novus*. Ed. Sonu Shamdasani. Trans. Mark Kyburz, John Peck, and Sonu Shamdasani. W.W. Norton & Company, 2009.

Kennedy, XJ, ed. *An Introduction to Poetry, Seventh Edition*. HarperCollins *Publishers*, 1990.

Kenner, Corrine. *Tarot for Writers*. Llewellyn Publications, 2009.

Klanprachar, Amnart and Thaworn Boonyawan. *Tarot Roots of Asia, Instruction Booklet*. Amaravati Publications, 1988.

Komachi, Ono No and Izumi Shikibu. *The Ink Dark Moon: Love Poems by Ono No Komachi and Izumi Shikibu, Women of the Ancient Court of Japan*, Translated by Jane Hirshfield with Mariko Aratani. Vintage Books, 1986.

Lande, Art. *Art Tarot, Instruction Booklet*. Art Lande, 2011.

Le Guin, Ursula K. *The Left Hand of Darkness*. Ace Books, 1981.

Lerner, Isha and Mark Lerner. *Inner Child Cards: a journey into fairytales, myth, and nature*. Bear & Company, 1992.

Masterson, Mark Anthony and David Maxine. *The Shadow of Oz: A Tarot Deck, Instruction Booklet*. Illogical Associates, 2014.

Matthews, Caitlin. *The Celtic Wisdom Tarot*. Destiny Books, 1999.

Morgan, Ffiona. Daughters of the Moon Tarot. Daughters of the Moon, 1984.

Murdock, Maureen. *The Heroine's Journey: Woman's Quest for Wholeness*. Shambhala, 1990.

Myss, Caroline. *Anatomy of the Spirit: The Seven Stages of Power and Healing*. Harmony, 1996.

Noble, Vicki. *Rituals and Practices with the Motherpeace Tarot*. Bear & Company, 1998.

…Motherpeace: A Way to the Goddess Through Myth, Art, and Tarot. Harper San Francisco, 1983.

Noble, Vicki, and Jonathon Tenney. *The Motherpeace Tarot Playbook: Astrology and the Motherpeace Cards*. Wingbow Press, 1986.

Pollack, Rachel. *Seventy-Eight Degrees of Wisdom: A Book of Tarot*. Element, An Imprint of HarperCollins *Publishers*, 1997.

…*Fortune's Lover: A Book of Tarot Poems*. A Midsummer Night's Press, 2009.

Pryputniewicz, Tania. *November Butterfly*. Saddle Road Press, 2014.

Two Sylvias Press. *Poet Tarot Guidebook: A Deck of Creative Exploration*. Two Sylvias Press, 2014.

Wanless, James. *Voyager Tarot: Way of the Great Oracle*. Merrill-West Publishing, 1989.

weiss, ruth. *a fool's journey: die reise des narren*. Translated by Peter Ahorner and Eva Auterich. Edition Exil, 2012.

ACKNOWLEDGMENTS

THANKS TO—

Ruth Thompson for sitting on a bench overlooking the ocean at Sea Ranch with me and saying, *Start somewhere. Pick a handful of cards.* Don, for your patience, exquisite eye, and steadfast care. My teacher Quan Tracy Cherry for the tarot apprenticeship in the heartland. Bonnie Orgren for the years of channeling, reiki, and astrology play in Iowa City. Longtime tarot buddy Mary Allen for the hours of "taroting" (Mary's term) in person, on the phone, and in dream.

Gillian Barlow, Carrie Nassif, and Lisa Rizzo for sharing your sacred art and the poetry of your insights— thank you for making this book possible.

Marni Freedman and the Feisty Writers— Lori Bessler, Phyllis Erickson, Anastasia Hipkins, Tanya Jarvis, Jen Laffler, Katie McNeel, Elizabeth Oppen, Kim Pierce, Nicola Ranson, Gina Simmons, Suzanne Spector, Barbara Thomson and Nancy Villalobos; especially Donna Agins who read multiple drafts and Lindsey Salatka for her skill. Tanya McDonald for her haiku expertise in the Tarot Haiku chapter; Penina Ava Taesali for connecting us. Robyn Beattie, Duane Deraad, Sandy Frank, Tina Pocha, Edith O'Nuallain, and Peter Pryputniewicz for unwavering belief in this book and your feedback. Corinne Stanley for the butterfly reading. Jamie Della for holding the mirror steady and showing up in so many ways. To the sweet believers, for their love—Vilma Baumann, Kathryn Meyer, Lydia Stewart, and Jerilynn Wagner.

The rest of the Flamingos— Jayne Benjulian, Sandra Hunter, Marcia Meier, Barbara Rockman, Michel Wing, and Barbara Yoder for flying with me.

The deck makers— William Cook Haigwood of the *Counterculture*, Isha Lerner and Mark Lerner of the *Inner Child Cards*, Two Sylvias Press of *Poet Tarot*, and Karen Vogel and Vicki Noble of *Motherpeace*.

The poets— Annie Finch, Tanya Ko Hong, Marianela Madranelo, Tanya McDonald, Christine Stewart-Nuñez, and with sorrow, the late ruth weiss we lost before she could hold the book in her hands. Tarot luminary Rachel Pollack for your poem and your years of beautiful tarot contributions.

My tarot students over the last twenty-seven years for your soul questions and your pathfinding answers. The Tarot Journalers at SDWI for facing the cards every week (especially tarot regulars Hayli, Heather, Hunter, Jill, Judy, Madonna, Nancy, and Thelma). My husband Mark and our children Kallista, Nik, and Orion for living with a kitchen table more often than not covered in colored pencils, tarot cards, and books. And last but not least, Todd Trask, for my silver queen; we couldn't ask for a better best man.

ABOUT THE AUTHOR

Tania Pryputniewicz is a heart-centered writing teacher, poet, and tarot muse passionate about inspiring others to engage in cross-pollination and hybrid forms from poetry movies to tarot haiku. Once trapped in a loveless romance in her early twenties as an undergraduate English Major, Tania found a tarot deck in a bookshelf that saved her soul and set her feet firmly on the Royal Road. She brings over twenty-five years as a writing teacher and practicing tarot reader to her tarot-inspired classes.

A graduate of the Iowa Writers' Workshop, Tania is the author of the poetry collection, *November Butterfly* (Saddle Road Press, 2014). She teaches poetry and tarot courses at San Diego Writers, Ink and through Antioch University's Center for Continuing Education and lives in Coronado with her husband, three children, one blue-eyed Siberian Husky and a formerly feral feline named Luna.

She blogs at *Tarot for Two* and at her main site— www.taniapryputniewicz.com.